USBORNE GUIDE TO WILD FLOWERS OF BRITAIN & EUROPE

BARRY TEBBS

Contents

Introduction	3
Flower Key	4
Types of Flower	5
Glossary	6
The Field Guide	8
Further Reading	124
Wild Plants and the Law	124
Index of English Names	125
Index of Scientific Names	127

Editorial Director Sue Jacquemier
Series Editor Rick Morris
Editor Jeff Cann
Designers Anne Sharples, David Bennett
Illustrators Hilary Burn, Joyce Bee, Edwina Keene
Additional artwork by Jill Coombs, Julie Piper, Ann Davies, Andy Martin, Paul Brooks

A number of the illustrations in this book have been previously published in the Usborne Spotter's Guides series and Usborne Regional Guides series.

First published in 1981 by Usborne Publishing Limited, 20 Garrick Street, London WC2E 9BJ

© 1981 by Usborne Publishing Limited

All rights reserved. No part of this publication may be reproduced, stored in a retrieval system or transmitted by any means, electronic, mechanical, photocopying or otherwise, without the prior permission of the publisher.

Printed and bound in Great Britain by Fakenham Press Limited, Fakenham, Norfolk.

Introduction

This book is a guide to the identification of some of the wild flowers of Britain and Europe, and is intended primarily for use in the field. The flowers are arranged by colour to make location and identification easier; there is a small heading at the top of each page that gives details of the colour and type of flower on that page.

The Illustrations

For each flower, there is a large colour illustration of the flowering part of the plant that often includes some other main feature such as the leaf. In addition, there is to the left of the page a more detailed illustration of the major distinguishing feature — this is usually the flower, but may also be an aspect of the leaf, stem or fruit if these are distinctive. To the right of the main illustration, a habit drawing illustrates the overall shape of the growing plant.

Measurements

Measurements are given in both metric and imperial terms, the imperial figure being the nearest convenient estimate to the more exact metric figure. The plant's height or the length of its stem is given next to the habit illustration. Flower and fruit sizes are given next to their illustrations.

The Text

The text underneath the main illustration gives details of alternative common names, the places in which the plant is likely to grow, its flowering time, whether it is annual, biennial or perennial and its geographical distribution in the British Isles. The text around the illustrations points out the main features of each plant to aid recognition. The text in the *Do not confuse* panel tells you how to distinguish the main plant from similar species with which it might be confused. The scientific names used are from *Flora Europaea* (ed. Tutin *et al*).

Plant Distribution

When used to describe a plant's distribution, the word *local* means that a plant is restricted to particular areas, or localised concentrations. These areas may themselves be restricted to specific regions or be distributed throughout the British Isles, and the incidence of the plant within its locality may range from common to rare. *Scattered* refers to plants that are not particularly common but are not found in specific concentrations — they are literally scattered over the stipulated areas. In order of decreasing abundance, flowers are described in this book as being *very common, common, fairly common, local, scattered,* or *rare*. Abundance is always related to habitat — even though a plant of open grassland is 'Common throughout the British Isles' it still would not be found in a mountain pine forest.

Variability in Plants

A factor common to all living things is their variability within the restrictions of their species. This is as true for the form and distribution of plants as it is for any other life form. The flower is the least variable part and is therefore the most useful for identification purposes. Leaf shape is more variable, and the overall habit depends greatly on the many aspects of the immediate locality. Therefore, although we show the most typical, be prepared for deviations from the specimens illustrated and the specific details given.

The Selection of Species

In selecting the species for this book, we have included examples of our rarer flowers, such as the Cheddar Pink and Red Helleborine, as well as our most common species, and thereby hope to provide a comprehensive guide to the beauty and variety of our flora.

Flower Key

The flowers in this book are grouped in eight major sections according to their colour. The flowers of each colour section are further arranged according to their form in the order of the categories illustrated below. Compare your specimen to the drawings in the left-hand column and then check the page numbers in the appropriate colour column. This will narrow the choice down to a few species and final identification is then easy.

	RED	PINK	PURPLE	BLUE	WHITE	GREEN	YELLOW	BROWN
0-3 PETALS	8	13			58-59	83-89	96	
4 PETALS	9	14-15	35	43-44	59-61	89-90	96-101	
5 PETALS	10-11	16-23	36	44-47	62-71	90-92	102-108	
6 or 6+ PETALS		24	36-37	48	71-73		109-112	122
COMPOSITE FLOWERS	12	25	37-39	48-50	74-76	93-94	112-116	123
LIPPED FLOWERS		26-28	39	51-53	76-77	94-95	117-118	
TUBULAR OR BELL FLOWERS	12	29-30	40	53-55	77-78			123
SPURRED FLOWERS		30-32	40-41	56-57			119	
PEA FLOWERS	13	33-34	42	57	79		120-121	
UMBELLIFERS					79-82		122	

Notes

The key is designed to provide an immediate visual guide and is not strictly confined to the scientific classifications of family.

The colours shown on the key are only representative — variations in hue do occur through each section. 'Mauve' flowers are included in either the pink or purple sections.

If a flower has a spur it is included in the *Spurred* category, regardless of its other features. The distinctively lipped Lizard Orchid (p95) is the one exception and it has been placed in the *Lipped* category, although it does have a small spur.

Types of Flower

For the purposes of this key the term 'petals' includes sepals and other petal-like structures where there are no true petals present. Each type of flower listed in the key (except umbellifers) may be found in different arrangements on different plants, from a solitary flower on a single stem (e.g. Hepatica *p48*, Silverweed *p102*) to many flowers in spikes and clusters of various shapes and densities (e.g. Rosebay Willowherb *p14*, Foxglove *p30*, Shepherd's Purse *p61*, Mountain Sorrel *p88*).

0-3 PETALS **Flowers with no petals or petals too small to be easily distinguished** (e.g. Sorrel *p8*, Caper Spurge *p83*, Cuckoo Pint *p88*) **and flowers with three easily distinguishable petals** (e.g. Flowering Rush *p13*, Water Soldier *p58*).

4 PETALS **Flowers with four easily distinguishable petals** (e.g. Field Poppy *p9*, Garlic Mustard *p60*, Woad *p100*).

5 PETALS **Flowers with five easily distinguishable petals** (e.g. Herb Robert *p20*, Dog Rose *p65*, Primrose *p107*).

6 or 6 + PETALS **Flowers with six easily distinguishable petals** (e.g. Purple Loosestrife *p24*, Fritillary *p37*, Snowdrop *p72*) **and flowers with more than six petals** (e.g. Lesser Celandine *p111*).

COMPOSITE FLOWERS **'Flowers' that are actually *flowerheads* made up of many very small flowers or *florets*** (see Glossary). This includes members of the family *Compositae* (e.g. Creeping Thistle *p38*, Daisy *p74*, Dandelion *p113*) and other plants with dense flowerheads (e.g. Teasel *p38*, Devil's Bit Scabious *p49*, Ribwort Plantain *p93*).

LIPPED FLOWERS
Upper lip
Lower lip

Flowers with two distinct lips. The upper lip is usually hooded to cover and protect the style and stamens. The lower lip usually has three lobes and is often patterned (e.g. Thyme *p28*, Self Heal *p52*, White Dead-nettle *p76*).

TUBULAR OR BELL FLOWERS
Fused corolla
Flowers whose petals are fused to form a tubular *corolla* (see Glossary). The tube may be long and straight (e.g. Foxglove *p30*), rounded (e.g. Bilberry *p12*) or bell-shaped (e.g. Harebell *p55*) and may be either curled back, lobed or slightly lipped at its open end.

SPURRED FLOWERS
Spur
Flowers with one of their petals extended to form a spur (e.g. Pyramidal Orchid *p32*, Larkspur *p56*, Wild Pansy *p119*). The spur often contains nectar to attract insects.

PEA FLOWERS
Standard petal
Wing petal
Keel petal

Flowers with a large, upper 'standard' petal, a 'wing' petal on either side and a lower 'keel' petal that contains the reproductive organs (e.g. Sainfoin *p33*, Hairy Tare *p57*, Broom *p121*). Sometimes pea flowers grow in dense heads (e.g. White Clover *p79*).

UMBELLIFERS
Umbel

Plants with umbrella-shaped flowerheads (called umbels) form an unmistakeable visual group (e.g. Cow Parsley *p80*, Wild Parsnip *p122*). This is the only category in the book based on the arrangement of the flower on the stem rather than on the form of the individual flower.

Glossary
The Flower

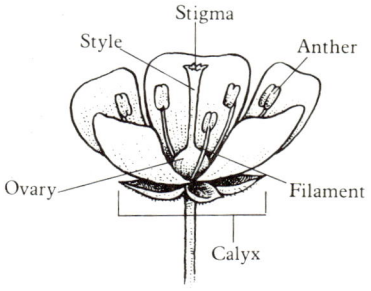
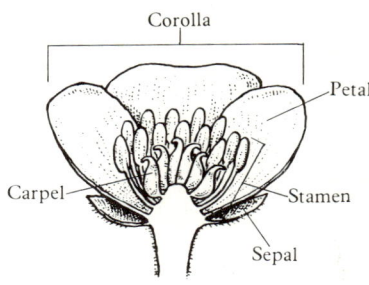

Anther: The part of the *stamen* on which the pollen is produced.
Bulbil: A small, bulb-like organ formed by the plant which, after separating from the parent plant, grows into another plant without being fertilised.
Calyx: Collective term for the *sepals*, especially when they are fused. They protect the flower bud and support the flower.
Carpel: The female reproductive organ comprising the *stigma*, *style* and *ovary*.
Corolla: Collective term for the *petals*, especially when they are fused.
Filament: The stalk of the *stamen* that supports the *anther*.
Ovary: The part of the *carpel* in which the eggs are produced.
Petal: A segment of the *corolla* — usually brightly coloured, sometimes absent.
Sepal: A segment of the *calyx* — usually green.
Stamen: The male reproductive organ comprising the *anther* and *filament*.
Stigma: The end surface of the *style* that receives the pollen grains.
Style: The part of the *carpel* between the *stigma* and the *ovary*.

Composite Flowers

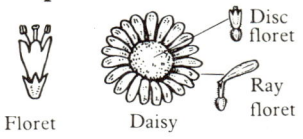

Floret — Daisy — Dandelion — Cornflower — Field Scabious — Thistle

Florets: Very small, simple flowers that form flowerheads.
   Disc floret: Floret with a regularly-shaped corolla found at the centre of a daisy-like flower.
   Ray floret: Floret with one side of its corolla extended to form a petal-like ray; found at the outside of daisy-like flowers. Dandelion-like flowers have only ray florets.
Florets form various types of flowerheads; examples are shown above.

Flowerhead: Dense cluster of florets that often looks like a single flower.

Plant Shapes (Habits)

Runner — Sprawling — Erect or upright — Shrub — Mat forming

The shape in which a plant grows is one of its chief characteristics. The major aspects of possible plant shapes are illustrated above.

Leaves

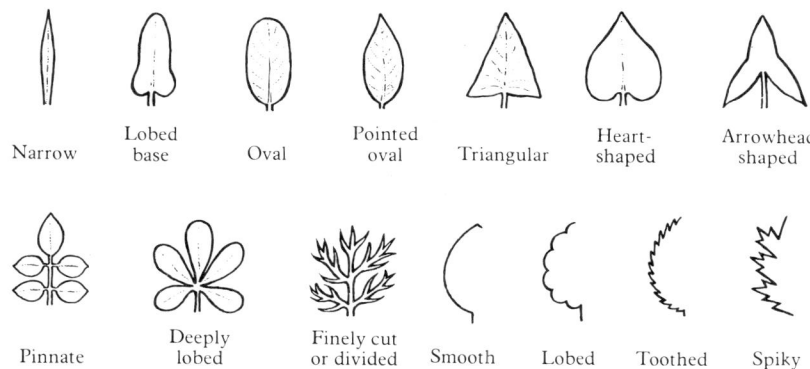

The leaf is often the second most important factor in plant recognition and can be the most important when the plant is not in flower. The many variations in shape are illustrated above. Each shape may have one or a combination of the four types of leaf edge illustrated here. **Compound leaves** consist of several leaf-like segments called **leaflets**.

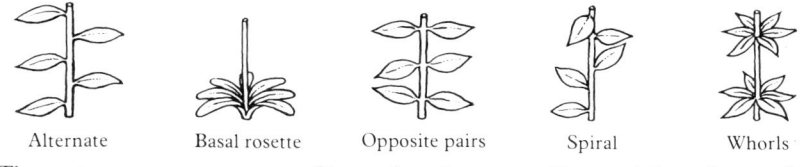

The most common arrangements of leaves along the stem are illustrated above. In any of the arrangements the leaves may be stalked or unstalked, and often a plant will have stalked leaves at the base and unstalked leaves towards the top.

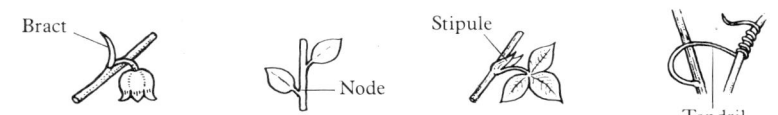

Bract: Leaf-like or scale-like structure at the base of a flowerhead or stalk.
Node: The point where the leaf meets the stem.
Stipule: Leaf-like or scale-like structure at the base of a leaf stalk.
Tendril: Modified stem, stalk or leaf used for climbing.

Life Span

Annual: Plant flowers and dies in one year.
Biennial: Plant lives for two years, usually flowering and dying in the second year.
Perennial: Plant lives for more than two years, usually flowering every year.

RED **0-3 PETALS**

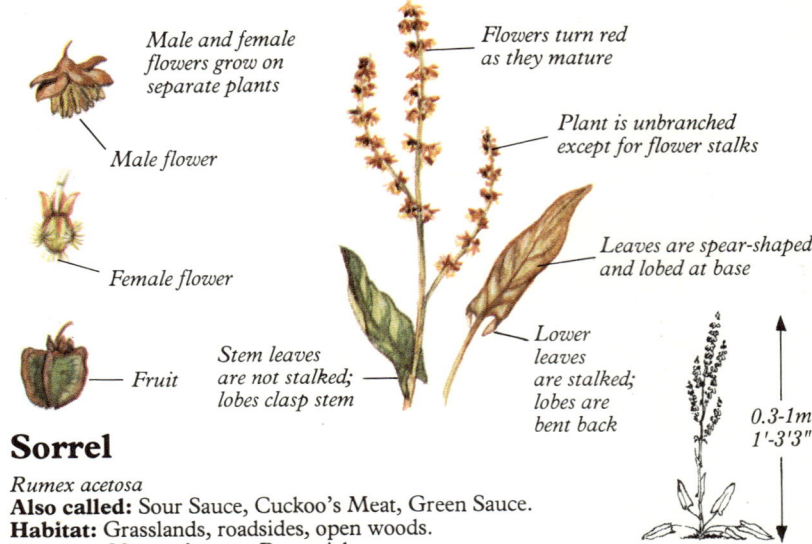

Sorrel

Rumex acetosa
Also called: Sour Sauce, Cuckoo's Meat, Green Sauce.
Habitat: Grasslands, roadsides, open woods.
Flowers: May to August. Perennial.
Distribution: Common throughout the British Isles.

Sheep's Sorrel

Rumex acetosella
Habitat: Heaths, grassland, sandy soils.
Flowers: May to August. Perennial.
Distribution: Common throughout the British Isles.

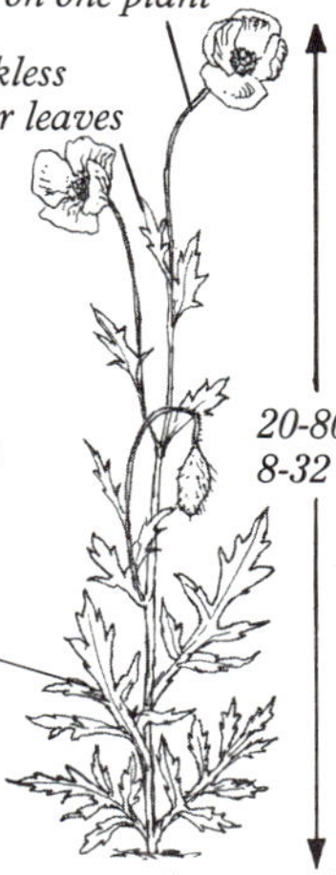

RED **4 PETALS**

Petals are roundish, often with black blotch at base

70-100mm
2.8-4"

Stems are usually branched, often with many flowers on one plant

Stalkless upper leaves

10-20mm
0.4-0.8"

Bluish anthers

Fruit (seed pod) is hairless; its length is not more than twice its diameter

Flower bud; sepals are hairy

Leaves are deeply divided and covered with stiff hairs

20-80cm
8-32"

Stem has stiff hairs

Field Poppy

Papaver rhoeas
Also called: Corn Poppy, Common Poppy.
Habitat: Corn and other fields, waste ground.
Flowers: May to August. Annual (rarely biennial).
Distribution: Common throughout the British Isles; but rare in northern Scotland and western Ireland.

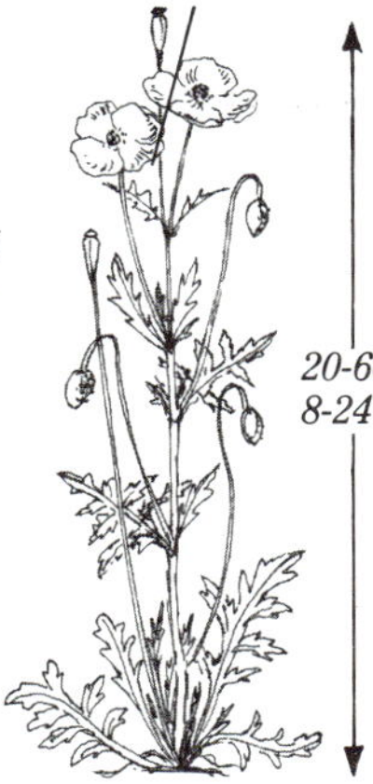

Basal leaves are stalked

Often covers large patches

Petals are orange-pink to scarlet

Anthers are usually shorter than style and stigma

30-70mm
1.2-2.8"

Stems are erect, usually branched, with stiff, flattened hairs

Deeply divided, hairy leaves

Seed pod is long, narrow and hairless; its length is more than twice its diameter

20-60cm
8-24"

Long-headed Poppy

Papaver dubium
Habitat: Corn and other fields, waste places.
Flowers: June to July. Annual.
Distribution: Common throughout the British Isles. More common in the north than the Field Poppy.

Often covers large patches

RED 5 PETALS

Flowers are usually solitary on long stalks

Flowers may also be pink or white

Fruits have a long beak (the 'Crane's bill')

25-30mm
1.0-1.2"

Petals are slightly notched at ends

Leaves are round, hairy and deeply cut

Stems have long hairs

Bloody Cranesbill

Geranium sanguineum
Habitat: Dry, grassy and rocky places.
Flowers: June to August. Perennial.
Distribution: Scattered throughout the British Isles but absent from much of Scotland and Ireland.

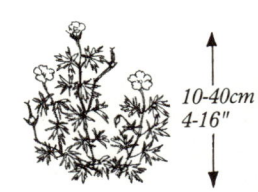

10-40cm
4-16"

Often a rather bushy plant

10mm
0.4"

Flowers are in small clusters

Bases of petals are enclosed by calyx

Flower has 5 petals

Do not confuse with *Green Houndstongue* which is smaller, less hairy, with green, shiny leaves.

Plant smells strongly of mice

Plant is covered with soft, grey hairs

Long, narrow stem leaves with silky hairs

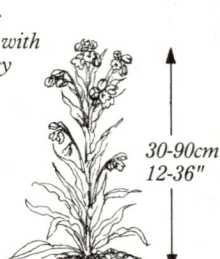

30-90cm
12-36"

Common Houndstongue

Cynoglossum officinale
Habitat: Dry, grassy places, especially near the sea.
Flowers: May to August. Biennial.
Distribution: Widespread but local throughout the British Isles, especially around the coasts.

Basal leaves are often withered when plant flowers

RED 5 PETALS

Leaves are in opposite pairs or whorls of 3

14mm
0.6"

Undersides of leaves are dotted with black glands

Flowers can also be blue

Stem is hairless and squarish

Petals have hairy edges

Flowers grow on long stalks from leaf nodes; they close in bad weather

6-30cm
2.4-12"

Scarlet Pimpernel
Anagallis arvensis
Also called: Poor Man's or Shepherd's Weatherglass.
Habitat: Cultivated and waste ground.
Flowers: May to September. Annual.
Distribution: Common throughout the British Isles.

Low, creeping plant; often covers large areas with stems hidden in grass

Summer Pheasant's Eye

Summer Pheasant's Eye has narrower petals that do not overlap.

Each petal has a dark spot at its base

15-25mm
0.6-1"

Single flowers grow at ends of branches

Seeds are in loose heads

Leaves are finely cut into narrow segments

10-40cm
4-16"

Pheasant's Eye
Adonis annua
Habitat: Cornfields.
Flowers: June to August. Annual.
Distribution: Grows wild mainly in southern England; rare in the wild elsewhere but is grown in gardens.

Upright, branched stem

RED COMPOSITE/TUBULAR OR BELL

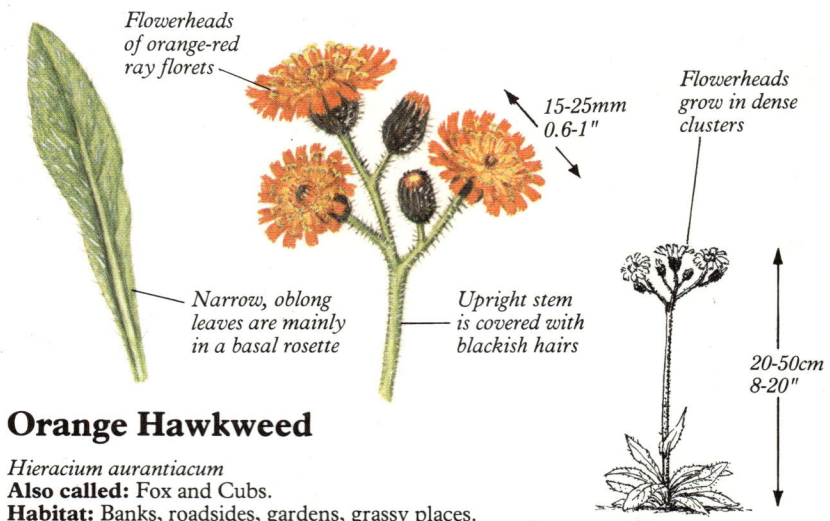

Flowerheads of orange-red ray florets

15-25mm 0.6-1"

Flowerheads grow in dense clusters

Narrow, oblong leaves are mainly in a basal rosette

Upright stem is covered with blackish hairs

20-50cm 8-20"

Orange Hawkweed

Hieracium aurantiacum
Also called: Fox and Cubs.
Habitat: Banks, roadsides, gardens, grassy places.
Flowers: June to August. Perennial.
Distribution: Scattered throughout the British Isles.

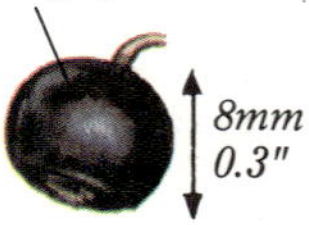

Rapidly forms quite large patches

Fruit is a black berry with grey bloom: edible

8mm 0.3"

Flowers are usually solitary and droop from leaf nodes

Calyx forms a cup

Stems are hairless and numerous; green when young

Corolla is an open tube with bent-back lobes

4-6mm 0.2"

Leaves are oval, pointed, toothed

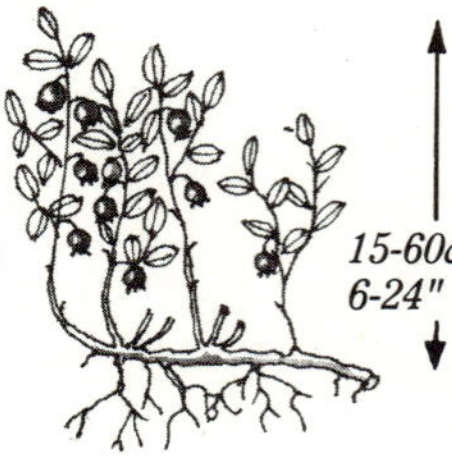

15-60cm 6-24"

Bilberry

Vaccinium myrtillus
Also called: Blaeberry, Whortleberry, Huckleberry.
Habitat: Heaths, moors, woods.
Flowers: April to June. Perennial.
Distribution: Common throughout most of the British Isles but rare in southern and central England.

Creeping root gives many upright stems

RED **PEA** PINK **0-3 PETALS**

Slender pea flower with low standard petal

9-15mm 0.4-0.6"

Calyx tube has bristle-like teeth

Heads look furry

Flowers grow in dense terminal heads

Leaves have 3 broad, oval leaflets

Plant is softly hairy

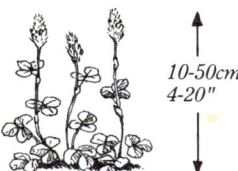

Do not confuse with *Red Clover* which has round flowerheads without protruding, bristly calyces.

RED CLOVER

Crimson Clover

Trifolium incarnatum
Habitat: Pastures, grassland; widely cultivated.
Flowers: May to September. Annual.
Distribution: Local, mainly in southern England.

10-50cm 4-20"

Plant is normally upright

Flower has 3 petals and 3 petal-like sepals

Flowers are on long, unequal stalks

3 dry, bract-like structures below flower stalks

2-3cm 0.8-1.2"

Leaves have 3 corners and grow from the roots

Stems are smooth and round

Flowering Rush

Butomus umbellatus
Habitat: By still and moving water, marshes, swamps.
Flowers: July to September. Perennial.
Distribution: Local in England and Ireland; rare elsewhere.

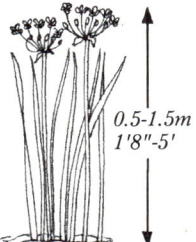

0.5-1.5m 1'8"-5'

Often forms large clumps

PINK **4 PETALS**

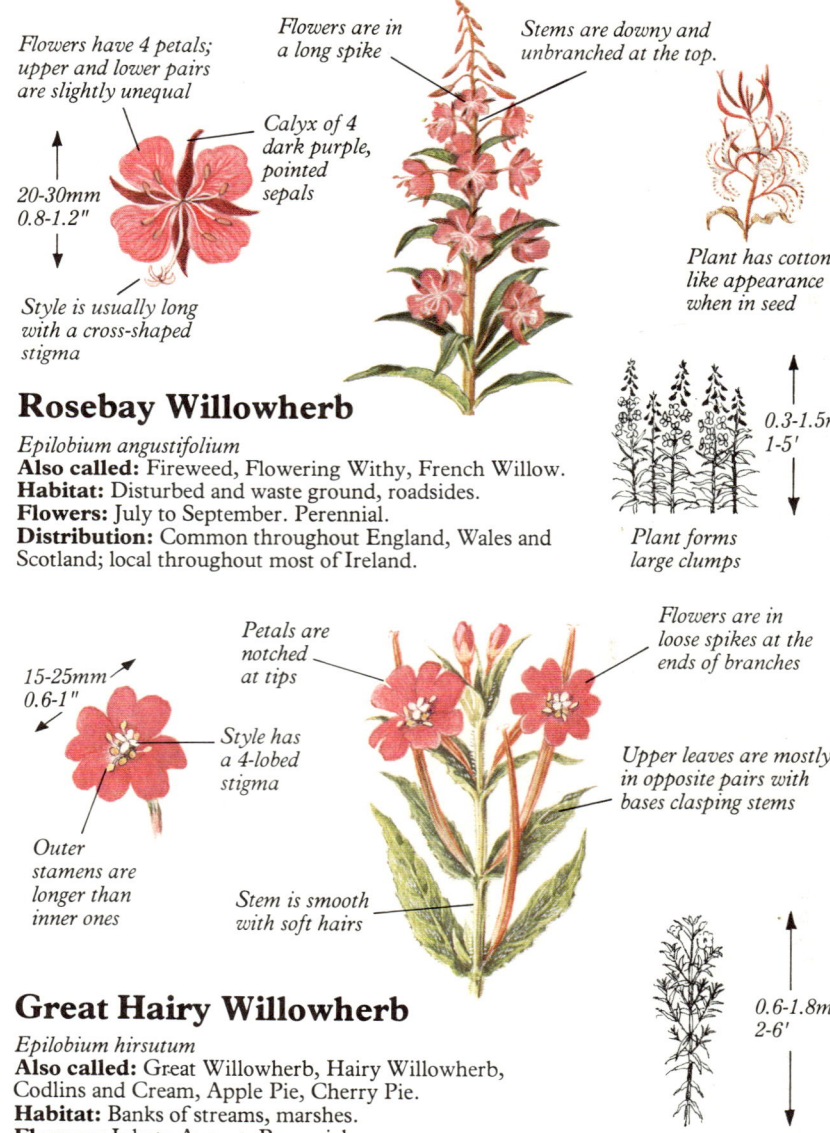

Flowers have 4 petals; upper and lower pairs are slightly unequal

Flowers are in a long spike

Stems are downy and unbranched at the top.

Calyx of 4 dark purple, pointed sepals

20-30mm
0.8-1.2"

Style is usually long with a cross-shaped stigma

Plant has cotton-like appearance when in seed

Rosebay Willowherb

Epilobium angustifolium
Also called: Fireweed, Flowering Withy, French Willow.
Habitat: Disturbed and waste ground, roadsides.
Flowers: July to September. Perennial.
Distribution: Common throughout England, Wales and Scotland; local throughout most of Ireland.

0.3-1.5m
1-5'

Plant forms large clumps

Petals are notched at tips

Flowers are in loose spikes at the ends of branches

15-25mm
0.6-1"

Style has a 4-lobed stigma

Upper leaves are mostly in opposite pairs with bases clasping stems

Outer stamens are longer than inner ones

Stem is smooth with soft hairs

Great Hairy Willowherb

Epilobium hirsutum
Also called: Great Willowherb, Hairy Willowherb, Codlins and Cream, Apple Pie, Cherry Pie.
Habitat: Banks of streams, marshes.
Flowers: July to August. Perennial.
Distribution: Common throughout the British Isles, except in the far north of Scotland.

0.6-1.8m
2-6'

Plant is normally branched at top

PINK **4 PETALS**

Small flowers grow in leafy spikes

Petals are shorter than calyx

Do not confuse with other *Heaths* and *Heathers* (p29) which have leaves that do not overlap and petals longer than the calyx.

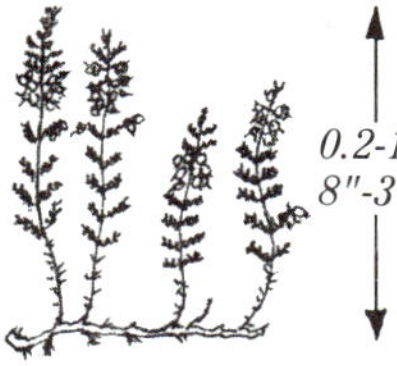

Long style and 8 stamens

Calyx is large and resembles the petals

Small, narrow leaves overlap in opposite rows

Stems are sometimes downy

Heather

Calluna vulgaris
Also called: Ling, Heath, Hadder, Hedder.
Habitat: Heaths, bogs, moors.
Flowers: July to October. Perennial.
Distribution: Common throughout the British Isles.

0.2-1m
8"-3'3"

Forms a dense carpet when young

Flowers can also be lilac or white

Sepals have violet tips

7-20 stalked flowers at top of stem

12-20mm
0.5-0.8"

Basal leaves have rounded leaflets

Flowers have 4 petals and yellow anthers

Stem leaves have very narrow leaflets

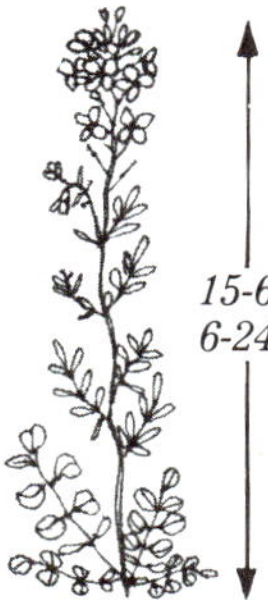

Cuckoo Flower

Cardamine pratensis
Also called: Lady's Smock, Milk Maids, Mayflower.
Habitat: Damp meadows, pastures, by streams.
Flowers: April to July. Perennial.
Distribution: Common throughout the British Isles.

15-60cm
6-24"

Plant is hairless

PINK 5 PETALS

8-15mm
0.4-0.6"

5 petals with ragged ends

Calyx is soft and hairy

Clusters of up to 10 flowers close in the afternoon

Flower buds

Leaves are pointed and in opposite pairs

Long, green bracts surround flowerheads

30-60cm
12-36"

Basal leaves form a rosette

Deptford Pink
Dianthus armeria
Habitat: Hedgerows, waysides, dry grassland.
Flowers: July to August. Biennial.
Distribution: Scattered throughout England and Wales; much rarer in Scotland and absent from Ireland.

Do not confuse with *Clove Pink* which has up to 5 flowers on each stem.

20-30mm
0.8-1.2"

Solitary flowers have 5 toothed petals

Flower bud

Flowers are strongly clove-scented

Bract-like scales surround base of calyx tube

Grey-green stem is smooth

Narrow leaves have slightly toothed edges

10-20cm
4-8"

Cheddar Pink
Dianthus gratianopolitanus
Habitat: Limestone cliffs.
Flowers: June to July. Perennial.
Distribution: Found in Cheddar Gorge and area; rare.

Plant forms large mats

PINK **5 PETALS**

10 white scales at base of petals

*18-25mm
0.7-1"*

Do not confuse with *Soapwort* (p21) which has paler, unnotched petals.

The 5 petals are deeply cut

Reddish calyx

Female flowers have 5 protruding stamens

Leaves are oval and in opposite pairs

Stem and calyces are softly hairy, often sticky

Male and female flowers grow on separate plants

*30-90cm
12-36"*

Red Campion

Silene dioica
Habitat: Well-drained woods, fields, hedgebanks.
Flowers: May to October. Perennial.
Distribution: Locally common throughout the British Isles, though it is rare in some areas.

Flowering and non-flowering shoots are produced

*30-50mm
1.2-2"*

Petals are notched and shorter than sepals

Stem leaves are opposite, hairy, narrow and pointed

Basal leaves are wider than stem leaves

Calyx tube is hairy with 5 long teeth

Stem is covered with flattened, white hairs

Corn Cockle

Agrostemma githago
Habitat: Cornfields.
Flowers: June to August. Annual.
Distribution: Rare throughout the British Isles.

*30-100cm
12-40"*

Stem has few branches

17

PINK 5 PETALS

Leaves are narrow and pointed

Flowers are in groups at ends of branches

30-40mm 1.2-1.6"

Ragged-looking petals have 4 deep lobes

Fruit is surrounded by calyx

Stem is branched, rough and slightly hairy

Calyx tube is reddish; 10 veins, 5 lobes

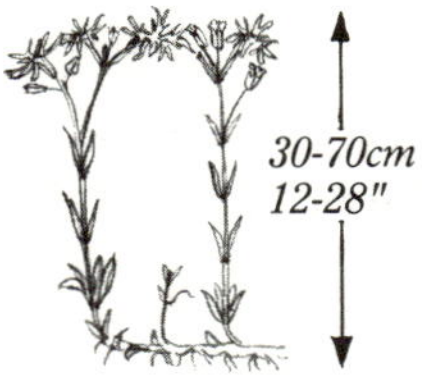

30-70cm 12-28"

Ragged Robin

Lychnis flos-cuculi
Habitat: Damp meadows, woods, marshes.
Flowers: May to August. Perennial.
Distribution: Common throughout the British Isles.

Flowering shoots are upright

Plant is hairless

10mm 0.4"

Corolla tube is longer than calyx

Do not confuse with *Slender Centaury* which has flowers on long stalks.

Flowers are usually in stalked clusters, seldom solitary

Stem leaves are in pairs and are distinctly veined

Common Centaury

Centaurium erythraea
Habitat: Dry, grassy places; dunes.
Flowers: June to October. Annual.
Distribution: Common in England, Wales and Ireland; rarer in Scotland and absent from the far north.

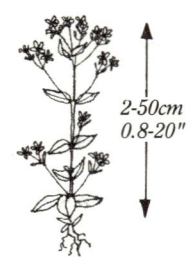

2-50cm 0.8-20"

Basal leaves form a rosette

PINK **5 PETALS**

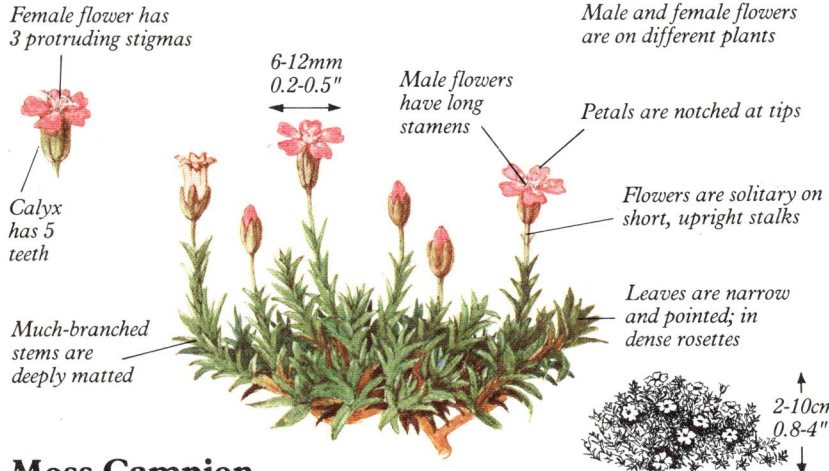

Many short, upright, flowering and non-flowering stems

5 oval petals

Small, oval leaves with hairy edges

Leaves are crowded on stems

Many long, creeping, rooting stems

10-20mm 0.4-0.8"

2-15cm 0.8-6"

Purple Saxifrage

Saxifraga oppositifolia
Habitat: Damp rocky and stony ground on mountains.
Flowers: March to May and August. Perennial.
Distribution: Local but often abundant in most mountainous areas of the British Isles.

Creeps and straggles over rocks; often forms large patches

Female flower has 3 protruding stigmas

6-12mm 0.2-0.5"

Male flowers have long stamens

Male and female flowers are on different plants

Petals are notched at tips

Calyx has 5 teeth

Flowers are solitary on short, upright stalks

Leaves are narrow and pointed; in dense rosettes

Much-branched stems are deeply matted

2-10cm 0.8-4"

Moss Campion

Silene acaulis
Habitat: Cliffs, scree, mountain ledges.
Flowers: June to August. Perennial.
Distribution: Mainly in Scotland and north Wales.

Forms distinctive bright green cushions; flowers are sometimes whitish

Do not confuse with *Pyrenean Cranesbill* which has less-cut leaves and deeply cut petals, or *Little Robin* which has smaller flowers.

Stems can be erect or sprawling

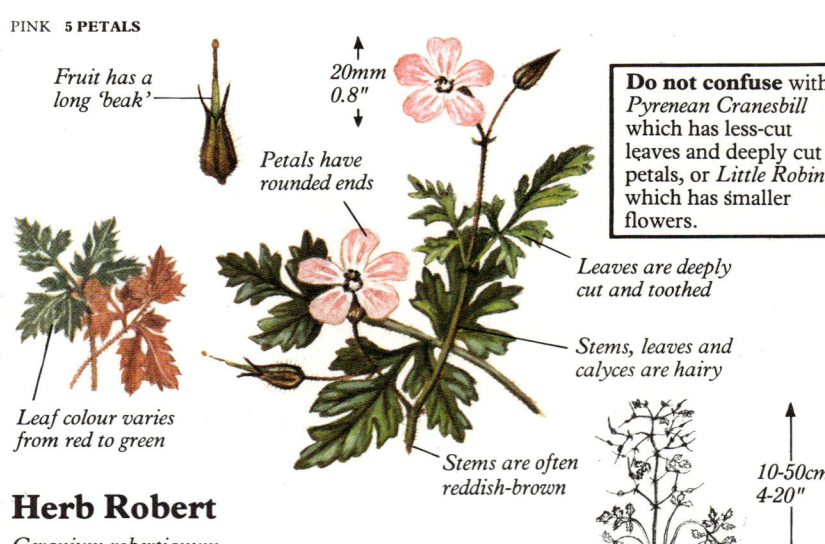

Herb Robert

Geranium robertianum
Habitat: Woods, hedgerows, rocks, in light shade.
Flowers: April to October. Annual or biennial.
Distribution: Common throughout the British Isles.

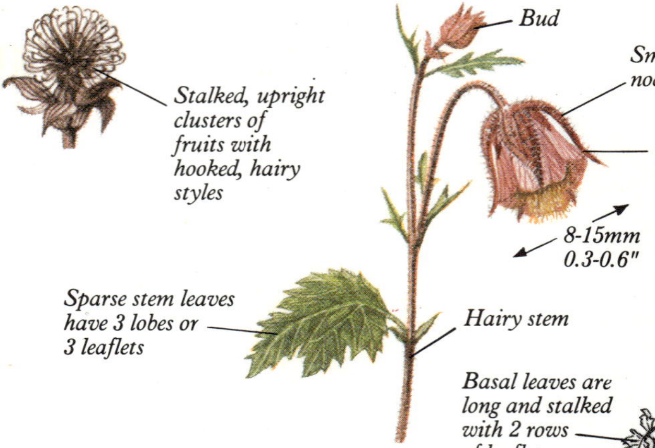

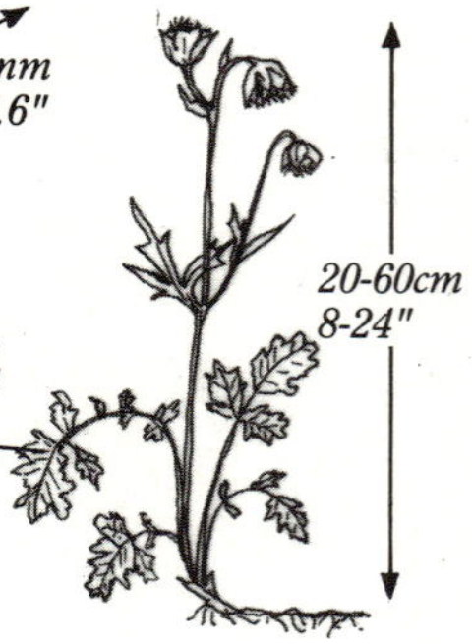

Soft, upright plant usually growing in shade

Water Avens

Geum rivale
Also called: Billy's Button, Granny's Bonnet, London Basket.
Habitat: Damp, shady places.
Flowers: May to September. Perennial.
Distribution: Common throughout most of the British Isles.

PINK **5 PETALS**

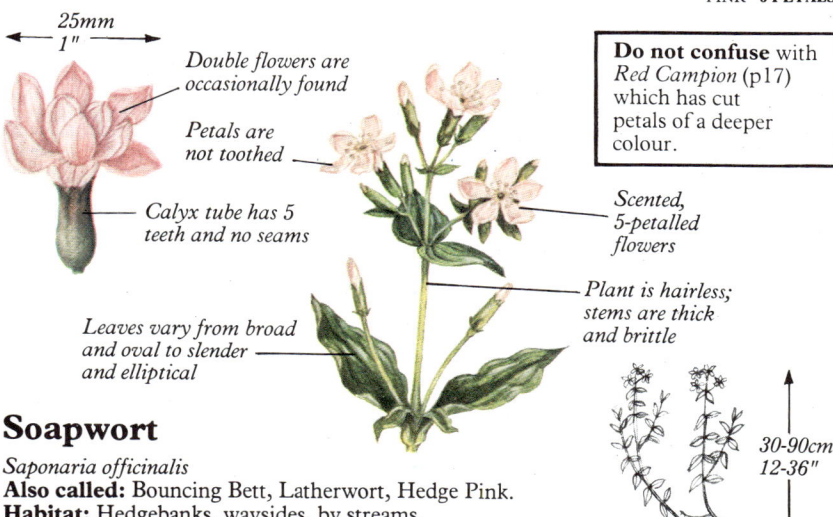

Do not confuse with *Red Campion* (p17) which has cut petals of a deeper colour.

Plant may form dense clumps

Soapwort
Saponaria officinalis
Also called: Bouncing Bett, Latherwort, Hedge Pink.
Habitat: Hedgebanks, waysides, by streams.
Flowers: June to October. Perennial.
Distribution: Fairly common throughout the British Isles except in the far north of Scotland.

30-90cm
12-36"

Do not confuse with *Musk Mallow* which has deeply cut leaves, or *Marsh Mallow* which has larger, pinker flowers.

Untidy, often scrambling plant

Common Mallow
Malva sylvestris
Habitat: Roadsides, waste ground.
Flowers: June to September. Perennial.
Distribution: Common throughout England; rare in north-western Scotland; local elsewhere.

0.3-1.2m
1-4'

21

PINK 5 PETALS

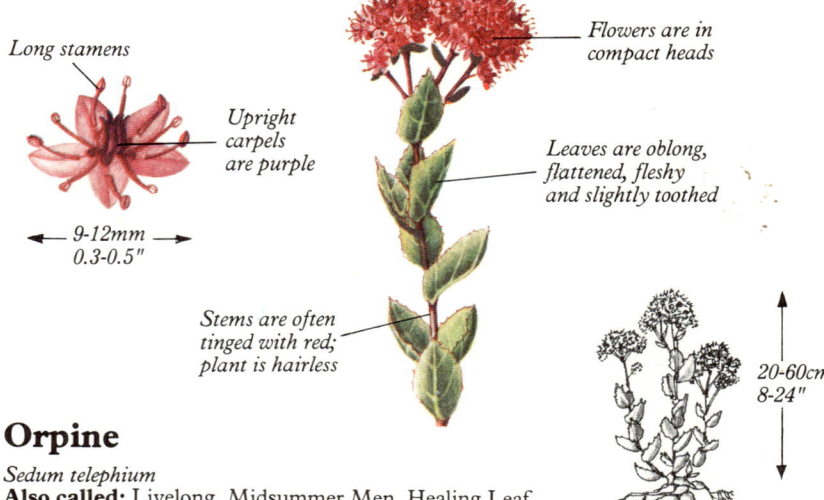

Long stamens

Upright carpels are purple

9-12mm
0.3-0.5"

Flowers are in compact heads

Leaves are oblong, flattened, fleshy and slightly toothed

Stems are often tinged with red; plant is hairless

20-60cm
8-24"

Stems are normally in clusters

Orpine
Sedum telephium
Also called: Livelong, Midsummer Men, Healing Leaf.
Habitat: Woods, shady places.
Flowers: July to September. Perennial.
Distribution: Scattered throughout the British Isles.

4-5mm
0.2"

Flowers have 5 petal-like sepals

Plant is almost hairless

Small flowers grow in a dense spike

Upper leaves clasp stem

Lower leaves are broader and stalked

20-80cm
8-32"

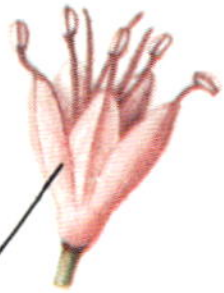

Often found in large patches

Bistort
Polygonum bistorta
Also called: Snake Root, Snake Weed, Easter Ledges.
Habitat: Grassy roadsides, meadows, near water.
Flowers: May to August. Perennial.
Distribution: Local throughout the British Isles; more common in the north of England; rare in Ireland.

PINK **5 PETALS**

Do not confuse with *Sea Spurrey* which has fleshy leaves with no bristles.

Petals are shorter than sepals

3-5mm 0.2"

Leaves are in pairs or whorls that have 2 silvery stipules

Small bristle at end of leaf

Leaves are narrow; not fleshy

5-25cm 2-10"

Sand Spurrey

Spergularia rubra
Habitat: Sandy, gravelly soil.
Flowers: May to September. Annual or biennial.
Distribution: Common throughout the British Isles.

Plant normally forms mats

Flower has 5 petal-like segments

1.5mm 0.06"

Flowers grow at bases of upper leaves

Stem is hairless and creeping

Silvery sheath around stem at leaf bases

Leaves are long, narrow and widely spaced

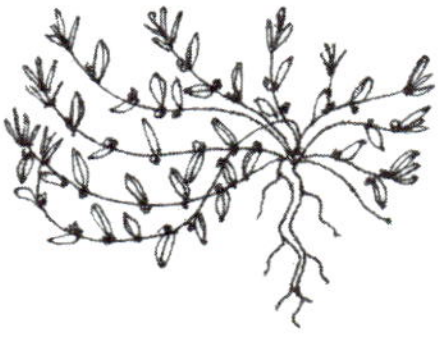

0.1-1.5m 4"-5'

Knotgrass

Polygonum aviculare
Habitat: Waste places, fields, sea shores.
Flowers: July to October. Annual.
Distribution: Very common throughout the British Isles.

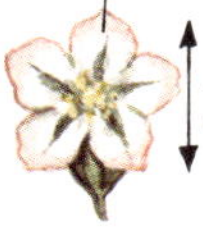

Usually low and far-spreading

PINK 6+ PETALS

10-15mm
0.4-0.6"

Plant is downy

Flowers are arranged in whorls on a spike of up to 30cm/12"

Lengths of stamens and styles are variable between plants

Leaves are narrow, long, with no stalk

Stem is squarish, upright, with 4 ridges along its length

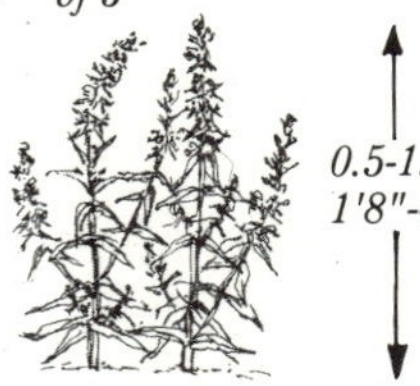

Lower leaves are in opposite pairs or whorls of 3

0.5-1.2m
1'8"-4'

Purple Loosestrife

Lythrum salicaria
Habitat: Wet places, by still and slow-moving water.
Flowers: June to August. Perennial.
Distribution: Locally common throughout England, Wales and Ireland; rarer in Scotland, especially the north.

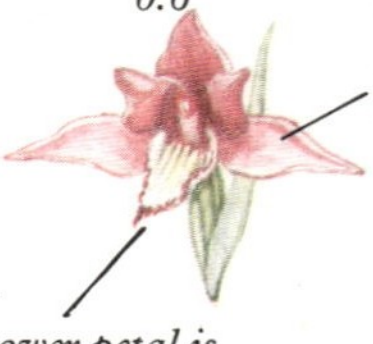

Plant often forms large colonies

15mm
0.6"

Outer petals have hairy outer surfaces

Bract

Lower petal is yellowish white and edged with violet, with a ridged inner surface

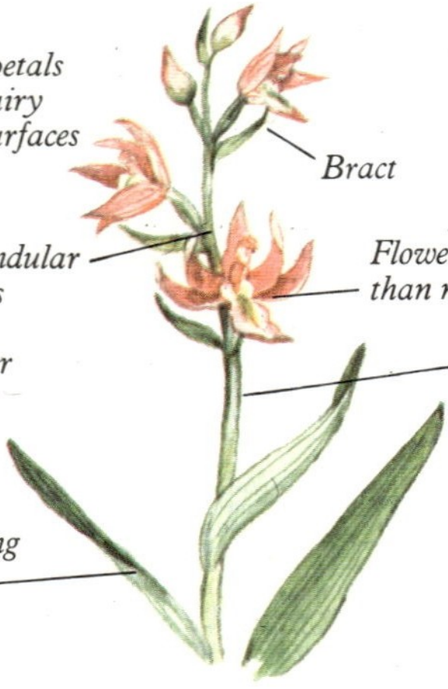

Glandular hairs on upper stem

Flowers are longer than narrow bracts

Stem often has a slight purple tinge

Do not confuse with *Dark Red Helleborine* which has broader leaves and more flowers on the usually more robust stem.

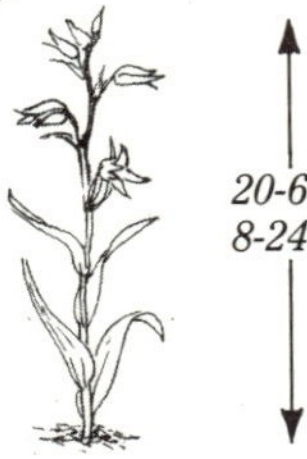

Leaves are long and narrow

Red Helleborine

Cephalanthera rubra
Habitat: Beechwoods on chalk or limestone.
Flowers: June to July. Perennial.
Distribution: Very rare throughout the British Isles but less so on the Continent.

20-60cm
8-24"

Plant often has leaves only

PINK   COMPOSITE

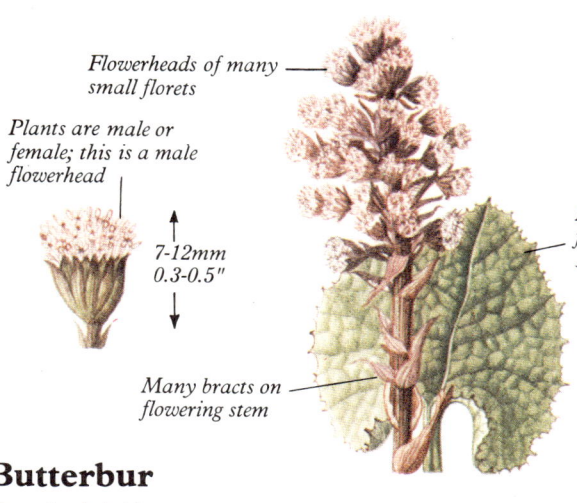

Flowerheads of many small florets

Plants are male or female; this is a male flowerhead

7-12mm
0.3-0.5"

Do not confuse with *Winter Heliotrope* which is scented and has smaller leaves and fewer flowerheads.

Leaves appear after flowers; up to 1m/3' across

Many bracts on flowering stem

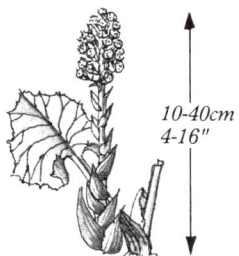

10-40cm
4-16"

Stem and flowerheads lengthen when fruit forms

Butterbur
Petastites hybridus
Habitat: Wet fields, copses, waste ground, by water.
Flowers: March to May. Perennial.
Distribution: Fairly common throughout the British Isles. The male is more common than the female.

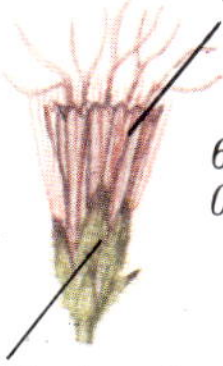

Each flowerhead has 5-6 florets

6-10mm
0.2-0.4"

Flowerheads are in dense, flat-topped clusters

Florets may be pink or white

Purple-tipped bracts below flowerheads

Stem leaves are usually unstalked with 3 toothed leaflets

Lined, downy stems are often reddish

Hemp Agrimony
Eupatorium cannabinum
Habitat: Stream banks, marshes, wet places.
Flowers: July to September. Perennial.
Distribution: Common throughout most of the British Isles; local to rare in Scotland and Ireland.

0.3-1.2m
1-4'

Upright, leafy plant

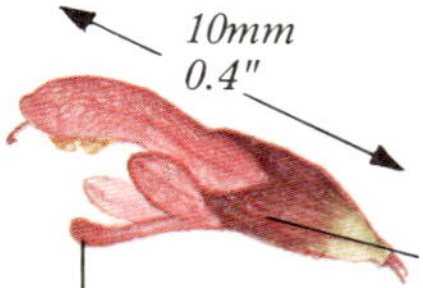

PINK **LIPPED**

10mm 0.4"

2-lipped corolla has a 3-lobed lower lip

Calyx tube has 4 teeth

Flowers usually droop to one side at top of stem

Plant is softly hairy, often with a purple tinge

Leaves are narrow, toothed, stalkless and in opposite pairs

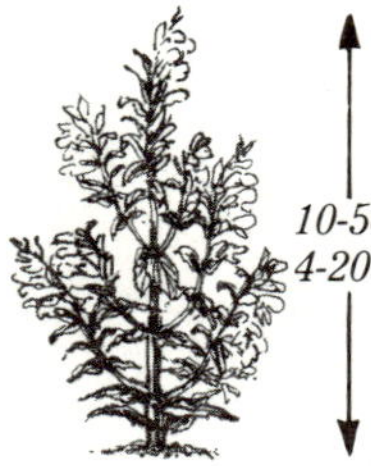

10-50cm 4-20"

Red Bartsia

Odontites verna
Habitat: Fields, waste places.
Flowers: June to September. Annual.
Distribution: Common throughout the British Isles.

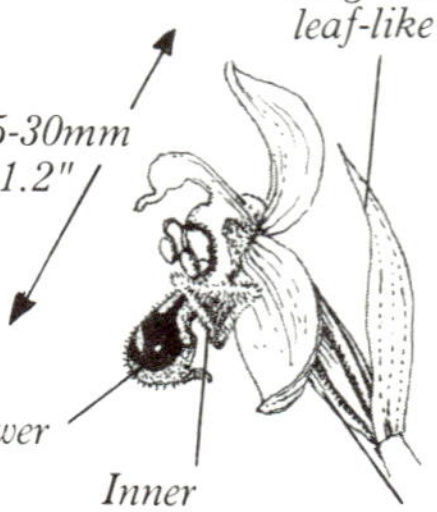

The plant is well branched

Bracts are long and leaf-like

Outer petal-like segments are pink on the front and green on the back

25-30mm 1-1.2"

Lower lip

Inner petal-like segment

The ovary is long and twisted

Do not confuse with *Spider Orchid* which has a larger, lobed lower lip, or *Fly Orchid*, which has a smaller, thinner, lobed lower lip.

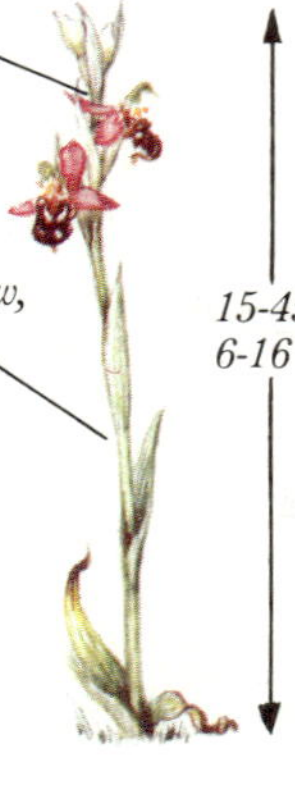

2-7 flowers are widely spaced in a long spike

Narrow, oval, widely spaced leaves

15-45cm 6-16"

Bee Orchid

Ophrys apifera
Habitat: Grasslands, open woods, scrub, disturbed ground.
Flowers: June to July. Perennial.
Distribution: Local in England; rarer in Wales and Ireland; absent from Scotland.

PINK **LIPPED**

Flowers are 2-lipped

Do not confuse with *Hedge (Wood) Woundwort* (p 39) which has dark purple flowers.

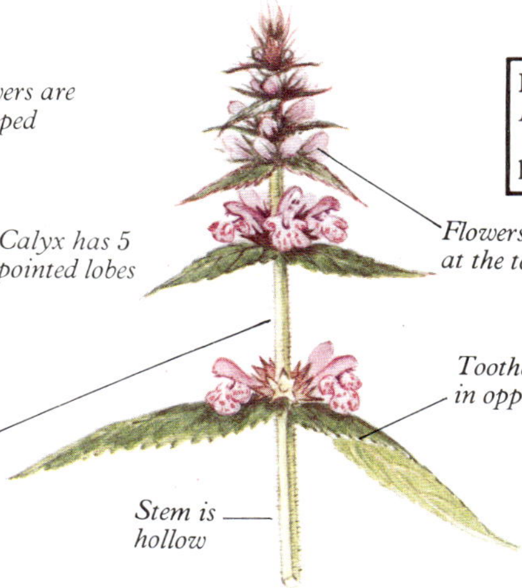

Calyx has 5 pointed lobes

12-15mm
0.5-0.6"

Flowers are in whorls at the top of the stem

Toothed leaves are in opposite pairs

Stem is hairy and more or less square

Stem is hollow

0.3-1m
1'-3'3"

Marsh Woundwort

Stachys palustris
Habitat: Wet, damp areas, by fresh water.
Flowers: July to September. Perennial.
Distribution: Common throughout the British Isles.

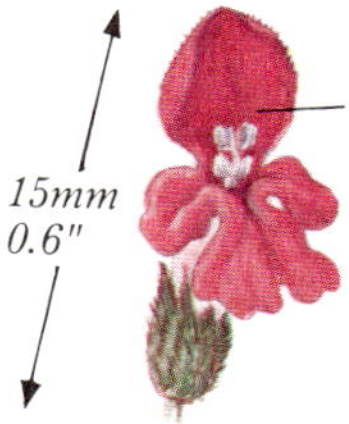

Stem is usually unbranched

Flowers are 2-lipped

15mm
0.6"

Flowers are in whorls that form a terminal spike

Plant is hairy; stem is usually unbranched

Topmost leaves have no stalks

Only 2-3 pairs of leaves on a stem

Lower leaves have long stalks

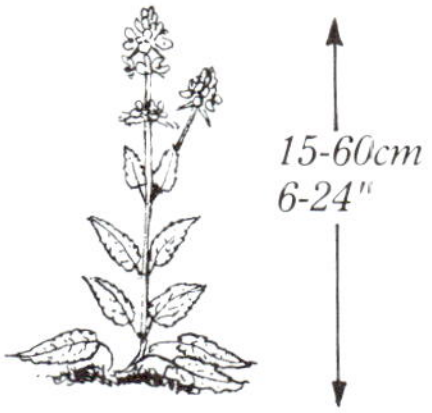

15-60cm
6-24"

Betony

Stachys officinalis
Habitat: Grassland, heaths, open woods, hedgebanks.
Flowers: June to September. Perennial.
Distribution: Common in England and Wales; rarer in Scotland and Ireland; absent from northern Scotland.

Most leaves form a basal rosette

PINK **LIPPED**

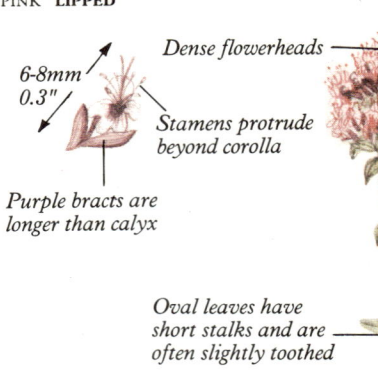

Dense flowerheads

6-8mm 0.3"

Stamens protrude beyond corolla

Purple bracts are longer than calyx

Do not confuse with many of the *Mints* which have similar flowers but a minty smell when crushed.

Pink, lipped flowers are much darker in bud

Oval leaves have short stalks and are often slightly toothed

Marjoram

Origanum vulgare
Also called: Wild Marjoram, Organy, Joy of the Mountain.
Habitat: Hedgebanks, grassy places.
Flowers: July to September. Perennial.
Distribution: Common throughout England and Wales; local in Ireland; rarer in Scotland.

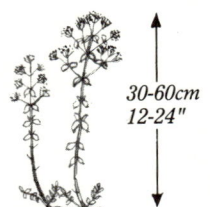

30-60cm 12-24"

Whole plant is pleasantly aromatic

Do not confuse with *Larger Wild Thyme* which is larger with a more elongated flowerhead.

Flowers are in rounded heads

4-7mm 0.2-0.3"

Stems are square and usually hairy on 2 sides only

Flower is 2-lipped

Creeping, rooting stems

Leaves are oval and often fairly woolly

Whole plant is strongly aromatic

Thyme

Thymus serpyllum
Habitat: Dry grassland, dunes, heath-like places.
Flowers: May to August. Perennial.
Distribution: Common throughout the British Isles.

5-10cm 2-4"

A small mat forming shrub

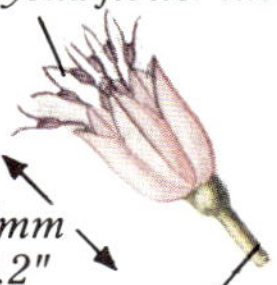

PINK **TUBULAR OR BELL**

Stamens project beyond flower tube

5mm 0.2"

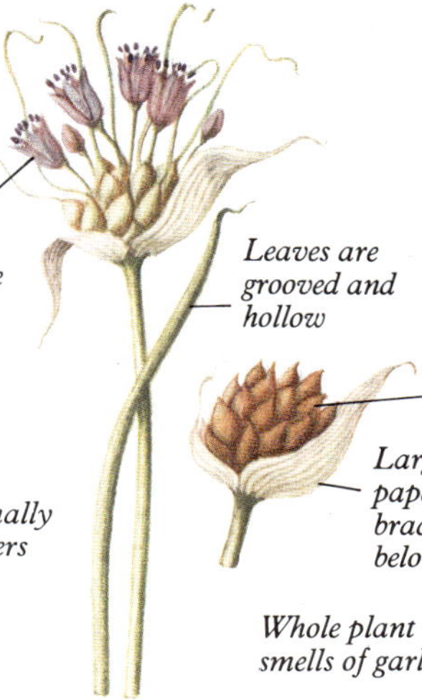

Flowers may be pink or greenish white

Leaves are grooved and hollow

Do not confuse with other *Garlics* which are smaller or have different coloured flowers, or *Leeks* which are usually larger with denser flowerheads.

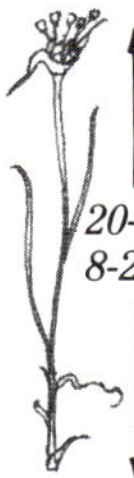

Flower stalks are longer than flowers

Bulbils are normally mixed with flowers

Flowerheads often have bulbils only

Large papery bracts below heads

Whole plant smells of garlic

20-70cm 8-28"

Crow Garlic
Allium vineale
Habitat: Fields, roadsides.
Flowers: June to August. Perennial.
Distribution: Fairly common and locally very common in England and Wales; local in Scotland and Ireland.

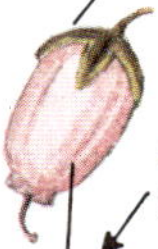

Stems are stiff and hairless

Flowers in short spikes

Calyx is smaller than corolla

5-6mm 0.2-0.3"

Plant is hairless

Bell-shaped corolla

Do not confuse with other *Heathers* and *Heaths*, especially *Cross-leaved Heath* which has whorls of 4 leaves and more compact flowerheads, and *Heather* (p15).

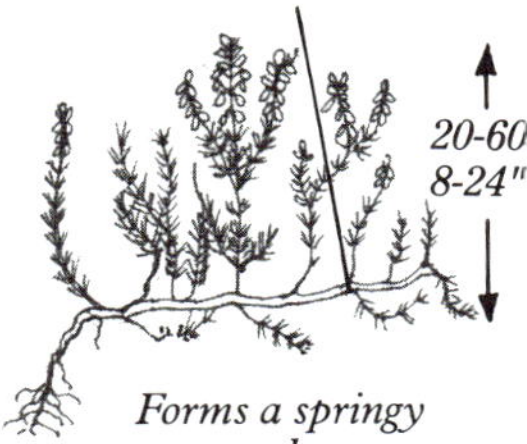

Whorls of 3 leaves

Tough, wiry stems root at their bases

20-60cm 8-24"

Bell Heather
Erica cinerea
Habitat: Drier areas of heaths, moors.
Flowers: July to September. Perennial.
Distribution: Common throughout the British Isles.

Forms a springy carpet when young

29

PINK **TUBULAR OR BELL/SPURRED**

*Plant is **poisonous***

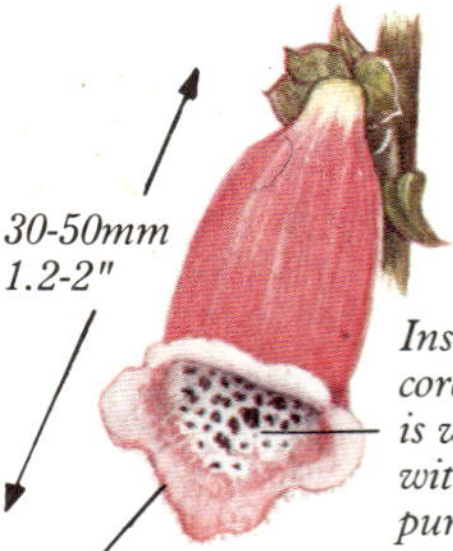

30-50mm
1.2-2"

Soft, grey hairs at top of stem

20-80 flowers droop to one side of stem

Inside of corolla is white with dark purple spots

Leaves are large and oval, with softly hairy upper surface and downy undersurface

Mouth of corolla has several long, white hairs inside

0.5-1.5m
1'8"-5'

Lowest leaves form a basal rosette

Foxglove

Digitalis purpurea
Also called: Fairy Gloves, Deadmen's Bells, Poppy Dock.
Habitat: Open woodlands, clearings, heaths, hedgerows.
Flowers: June to September. Biennial, rare perennial.
Distribution: Common throughout most of the British Isles

7-9mm
0.3"

10-40 flowers in a loose spike

Each flower has a spur

Tube-shaped flower is purple-tipped

Do not confuse with *Wall Fumitory* which is a larger, climbing plant, *Ramping Fumitory* which has white flowers, or with the smaller *Small Fumitory*.

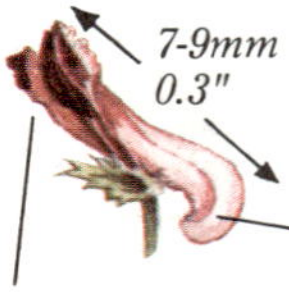

Bracts are shorter than fruit stalks

Feathery leaves are much divided

Plant is hairless; often grey-green

10-50cm
4-20"

Common Fumitory

Fumaria officinalis
Habitat: Cultivated, disturbed, or waste ground.
Flowers: April to October. Annual.
Distribution: Common throughout the British Isles.

A scrambling plant; often many together

PINK SPURRED

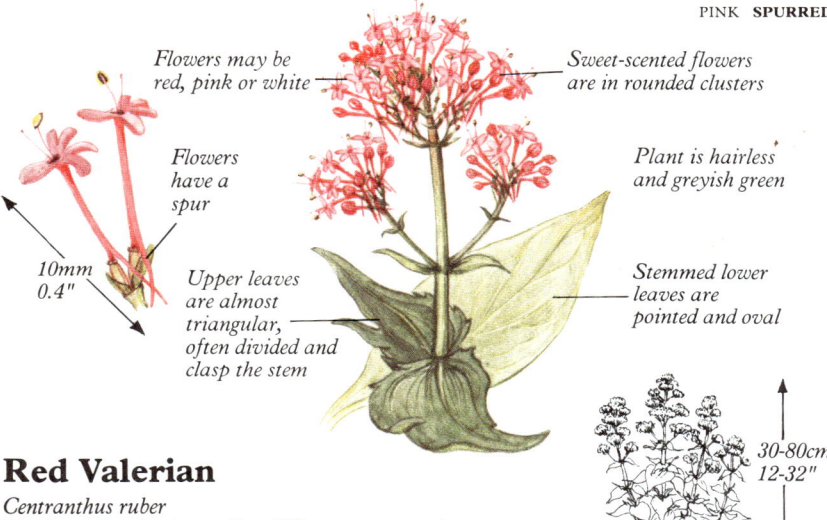

Flowers may be red, pink or white

Sweet-scented flowers are in rounded clusters

Flowers have a spur

Plant is hairless and greyish green

10mm
0.4"

Upper leaves are almost triangular, often divided and clasp the stem

Stemmed lower leaves are pointed and oval

Red Valerian
Centranthus ruber
Habitat: Dry banks, walls, cliffs, waste ground.
Flowers: May to September. Perennial.
Distribution: Fairly common throughout the southern British Isles but decreasing greatly northwards.

30-80cm
12-32"

Plant is tufted with many flowering stems

Stalked flowers have 3 petal-like sepals

Lower sepal has a short, bent spur

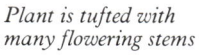

Do not confuse with *Orange Balsam* which has smaller, orange flowers, or *Wild (Touch-me-not) Balsam* which has yellow flowers.

2.5-4cm
1.0-1.6"

Seed pods explode when touched

Toothed leaves are in opposite pairs or in threes

Stout, hairless stems

Policeman's Helmet
Impatiens glandulifera
Also called: Himalayan Balsam, Indian Balsam.
Habitat: River banks, waste places.
Flowers: July to October. Annual.
Distribution: Locally common throughout England and Wales; rarer in Ireland and Scotland.

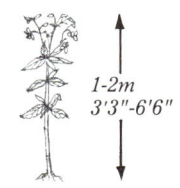

1-2m
3'3"-6'6"

Often forms clumps

PINK **SPURRED**

6-12mm
0.2-0.5"

Top petals form a hood

Each flower has a long, curved, narrow spur

Flowers are in a distinctly conical spike

Do not confuse with *Fragrant (Scented) Orchid* which has an elongated spike and scented leaves, or *Common Spotted Orchid* which has spotted leaves and flowers.

Leaves are unspotted

Upper leaves are smaller and pointed

Lower leaves wither at tip

20-60cm
8-24"

Pyramidal Orchid

Anacamptis pyramidalis
Habitat: Dunes, dry grassland.
Flowers: June to August. Perennial.
Distribution: Locally common throughout England and Ireland; rarer in Wales and very rare in Scotland.

Upper lobes form a hood

20-25mm
0.8-1"

Cylindrical spur is straight or curved upwards; as long as ovary

Lower lip is mottled; has 3 shallow lobes

Flowers are in a loose spike

Plant sometimes smells strongly of tomcats

Leaves are narrowly oblong, with many black-purple blotches

20-60cm
8-24"

Early Purple Orchid

Orchis mascula
Also called: Crowfoot, Cuckoo, Blue Butcher.
Habitat: Woods, copses, pastures, shady places.
Flowers: April to June. Perennial.
Distribution: Fairly common throughout the British Isles.

Single, upright stem

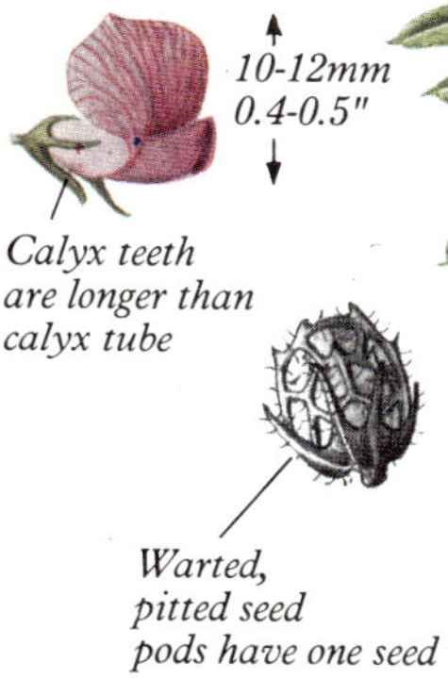

PINK **PEA**

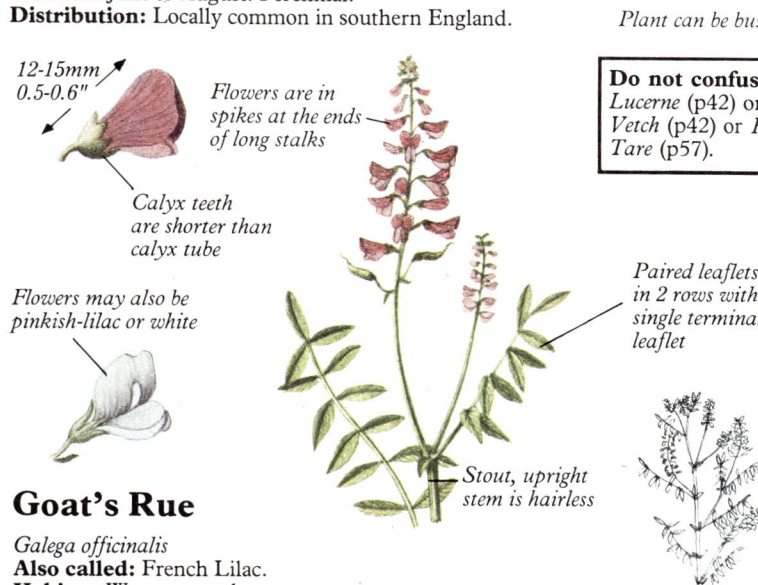

Flowers grow in a long, dense spike

10-12mm
0.4-0.5"

Calyx teeth are longer than calyx tube

13-15 leaflets

Warted, pitted seed pods have one seed

Long flower stem

Stem is slightly hairy

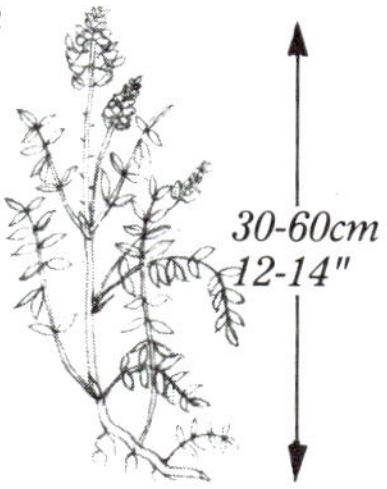

30-60cm
12-14"

Sainfoin

Onobrychis viciifolia
Habitat: Grassy places on chalk and limestone.
Flowers: June to August. Perennial.
Distribution: Locally common in southern England.

Plant can be bushy

12-15mm
0.5-0.6"

Flowers are in spikes at the ends of long stalks

Do not confuse with *Lucerne* (p42) or *Tufted Vetch* (p42) or *Hairy Tare* (p57).

Calyx teeth are shorter than calyx tube

Flowers may also be pinkish-lilac or white

Paired leaflets are in 2 rows with single terminal leaflet

Stout, upright stem is hairless

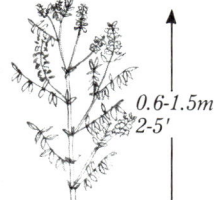

0.6-1.5m
2-5'

Goat's Rue

Galega officinalis
Also called: French Lilac.
Habitat: Waste ground.
Flowers: June to July. Perennial.
Distribution: Fairly common throughout the British Isles.

Plant is erect

33

PINK **PEA**

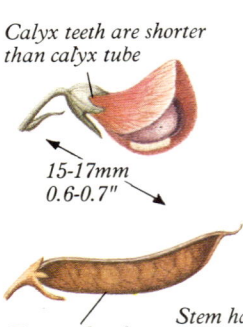

Calyx teeth are shorter than calyx tube

15-17mm
0.6-0.7"

Flattened pods

Stem has broad wings on either side

Do not confuse with *Everlasting Pea* which has larger flowers and broader leaves.

Flowers are in loose, long-stalked spikes

Long, narrow leaflets are in pairs

Tendrils

Narrow-leaved Everlasting Pea

Lathyrus sylvestris
Also called: Wild Pea.
Habitat: Woods, hedges, waste ground.
Flowers: June to August. Perennial.
Distribution: Locally common in England and Wales; absent from the north of Scotland and Ireland.

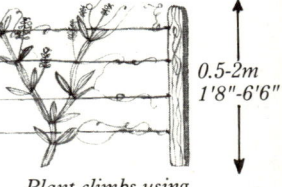

0.5-2m
1'8"-6'6"

Plant climbs using twining tendrils

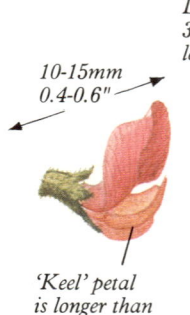

Leaves have 3 toothed leaflets

10-15mm
0.4-0.6"

Normally spiny

'Keel' petal is longer than 'wing' petals

Do not confuse with *Common Rest-harrow* which is creeping, and spineless, with wing petals longer than keel petals.

Flowers grow from leaf node

30-60cm
12-24"

Spiny Rest-harrow

Ononis spinosa
Habitat: Rough, grassy places.
Flowers: June to September. Perennial.
Distribution: Scattered throughout England; rarer in Wales; rare in Scotland; absent from Ireland.

Stems are upright with two lines of hairs along them

PURPLE **4 PETALS**

Petals sometimes have a dark blotch at base

80-180mm 3-7"

Flower colour varies from lilac to white. This is a sub-species of the oriental poppy from which opium is extracted.

Bluish anthers

Buds hang down

2-3cm 0.8-1.2"

Seed capsule

Leaves are greyish, large and wavy; upper leaves clasp stem

0.3-1cm 1'-3'3"

Opium Poppy

Papaver somniferum
Habitat: Waste ground, gardens.
Flowers: July to August. Annual.
Distribution: Scattered throughout the British Isles.

Plant often occurs in large numbers

Tiny, purplish flowers grow in umbrella-shaped heads

Fruits are red berries

10-25mm 0.4-0.8"

White bracts

Petal-like bracts below flowerhead

Elliptical leaves have marked veins

Single flower (much enlarged)

Plant is short and creeping, with upright stems

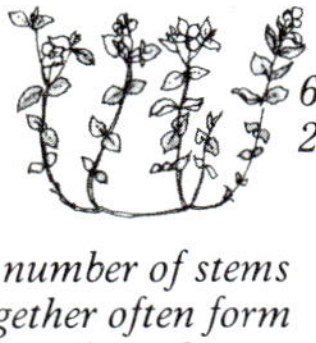

Dwarf Cornel

Cornus suecica
Habitat: Mountain moorland.
Flowers: July to August. Perennial.
Distribution: Locally common in north-western Scotland; very rare in England; absent elsewhere.

6-20cm 2.4-8"

A number of stems together often form a small patch

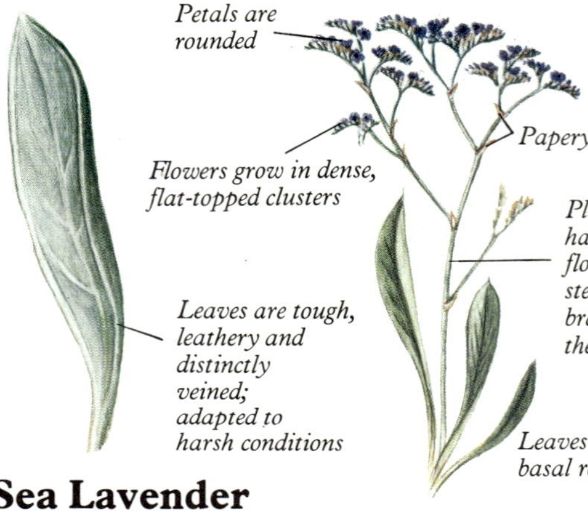

PURPLE 5 PETALS/6 + PETALS

Petals are rounded

Flowers grow in dense, flat-topped clusters

Papery bracts

Plant is hairless; flowering stems branch above their middle

Leaves are tough, leathery and distinctly veined; adapted to harsh conditions

Leaves are in a basal rosette

5-15cm
2-6"

Do not confuse with *Lax-flowered Sea Lavender* which branches from below the middle of the stem and has indistinctly veined leaves.

Sea Lavender

Limonium vulgare
Habitat: Muddy saltmarshes, coasts, estuaries.
Flowers: July to October. Perennial.
Distribution: Common around English and Welsh coasts but absent from Ireland, north and central Scotland.

Plant often forms large mats

50-80mm
2-3"

Solitary flowers are upright at first, droop later

Flower has no petals but 6 coloured, hairy sepals

Stalkless stem leaves are very finely divided

Whole plant is softly hairy

Each seed of the dense fruiting head has a long silky plume

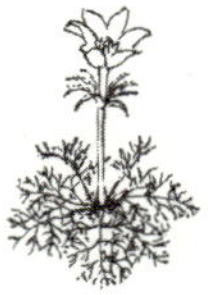

Pasque Flower

Pulsatilla vulgaris
Habitat: Dry, grassy, slopes.
Flowers: April to May. Perennial.
Distribution: Very rare; only in central England.

Each plant has a single flowering stem

7-23cm
3-9"

Feathery basal leaves form a rosette

PURPLE 6 + PETALS/COMPOSITE

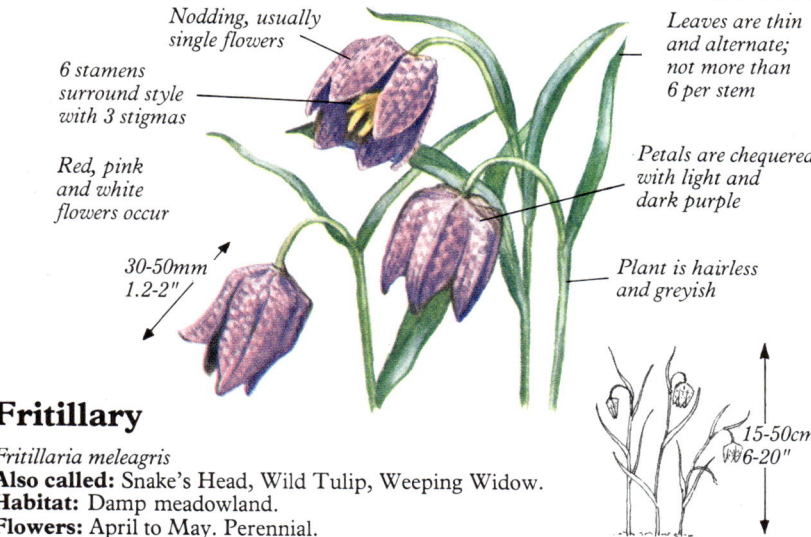

Nodding, usually single flowers

6 stamens surround style with 3 stigmas

Red, pink and white flowers occur

30-50mm
1.2-2"

Leaves are thin and alternate; not more than 6 per stem

Petals are chequered with light and dark purple

Plant is hairless and greyish

15-50cm
6-20"

Many plants often grow close together

Fritillary

Fritillaria meleagris
Also called: Snake's Head, Wild Tulip, Weeping Widow.
Habitat: Damp meadowland.
Flowers: April to May. Perennial.
Distribution: Mainly in the southern counties of England; it is now very rare in the British Isles.

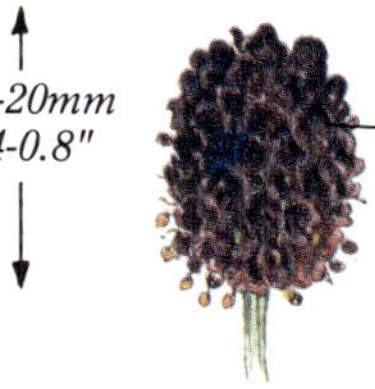

Flowers are clustered into oblong heads

10-20mm
0.4-0.8"

Tiny flowers have 4 petal-like sepals

Stem is upright and branched

Leaves have 2-5 toothed leaflets and are sparse on stem

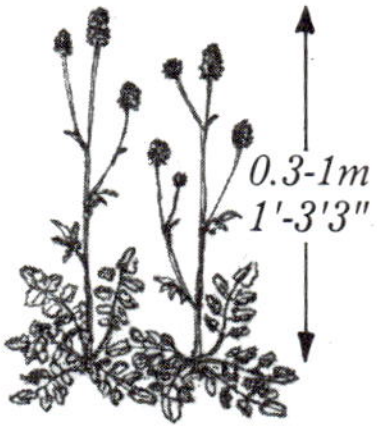

Great Burnet

Sanguisorba officinalis
Habitat: Damp grassland.
Flowers: June to September. Perennial.
Distribution: Locally common in northern and central England; rare elsewhere; absent from northern Scotland.

0.3-1m
1'-3'3"

Plant is hairless

PURPLE COMPOSITE

Spiny heads persist after flowers

*3-8cm
1.2-3.2"*

Florets in dense, upright, spiny heads

Flowers open in bands around flowerhead

Upward-curving prickly bracts surround flowerhead

Stem is hairless, angular, prickly

Only stem leaves are visible when plant is in flower

Leaf bases join around stem forming a water-collecting cup.

Leaves are prickly along mid-rib underneath

*0.5-2m
1'8"-6'6"*

Teasel

Dipsacus fullonum
Habitat: Roadsides, rough pasture, waste ground.
Flowers: July to August. Biennial.
Distribution: Locally common throughout the British Isles, becoming rarer northwards; absent from the far north.

Leaves of basal rosette die before plant flowers

*1.5-2.5cm
0.6-1"*

Flowerheads are on short stalks; solitary or in clusters of 2-4

Seeding head

All leaves have sharp spines

Florets

Purplish bracts

Lower leaves have short, stalk-like bases

Often the most common garden weed of the many thistles

Stems have no spines

Stem leaves clasp stem

*0.3-1.5m
1-5'*

Creeping Thistle

Cirsium arvense.
Also called: Field Thistle.
Habitat: Waysides, waste ground, fields.
Flowers: July to September. Perennial.
Distribution: Common throughout the British Isles.

Flowering and non-flowering stems are produced

38

PURPLE COMPOSITE/LIPPED

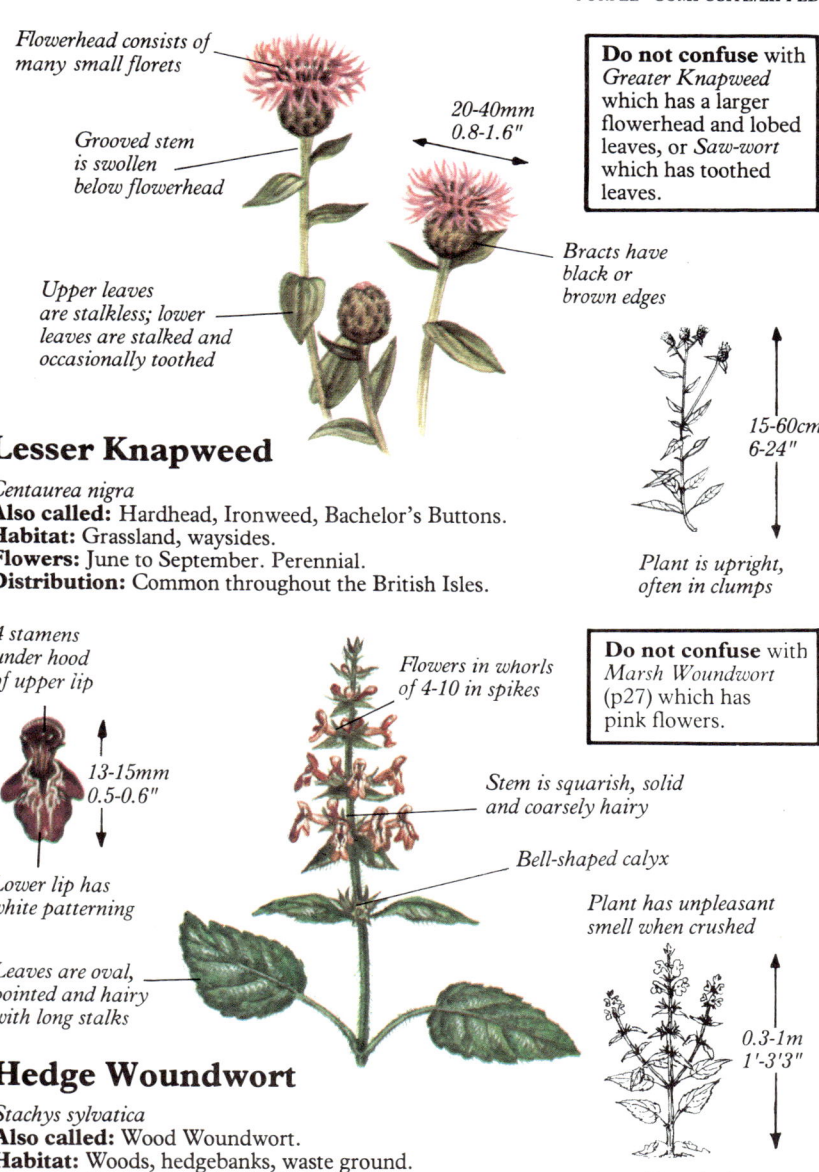

Flowerhead consists of many small florets

Grooved stem is swollen below flowerhead

20-40mm
0.8-1.6"

Do not confuse with *Greater Knapweed* which has a larger flowerhead and lobed leaves, or *Saw-wort* which has toothed leaves.

Upper leaves are stalkless; lower leaves are stalked and occasionally toothed

Bracts have black or brown edges

15-60cm
6-24"

Plant is upright, often in clumps

Lesser Knapweed

Centaurea nigra
Also called: Hardhead, Ironweed, Bachelor's Buttons.
Habitat: Grassland, waysides.
Flowers: June to September. Perennial.
Distribution: Common throughout the British Isles.

4 stamens under hood of upper lip

13-15mm
0.5-0.6"

Lower lip has white patterning

Flowers in whorls of 4-10 in spikes

Do not confuse with *Marsh Woundwort* (p27) which has pink flowers.

Stem is squarish, solid and coarsely hairy

Bell-shaped calyx

Plant has unpleasant smell when crushed

Leaves are oval, pointed and hairy with long stalks

0.3-1m
1'-3'3"

Hedge Woundwort

Stachys sylvatica
Also called: Wood Woundwort.
Habitat: Woods, hedgebanks, waste ground.
Flowers: June to September. Perennial.
Distribution: Common throughout the British Isles.

Plant is often well branched

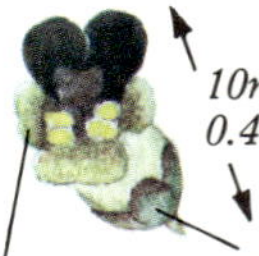

PURPLE **TUBULAR/SPURRED**

Common Figwort

Scrophularia nodosa
Also called: Figwort, Stinking Roger, Brownwort.
Habitat: Damp woods, hedgebanks.
Flowers: June to September. Perennial.
Distribution: Common throughout the British Isles.

Common Butterwort

Pinguicula vulgaris
Habitat: Bogs and wet rocks.
Flowers: May to July. Perennial.
Distribution: Common throughout the British Isles except in southern England and southern Ireland.

PURPLE **SPURRED**

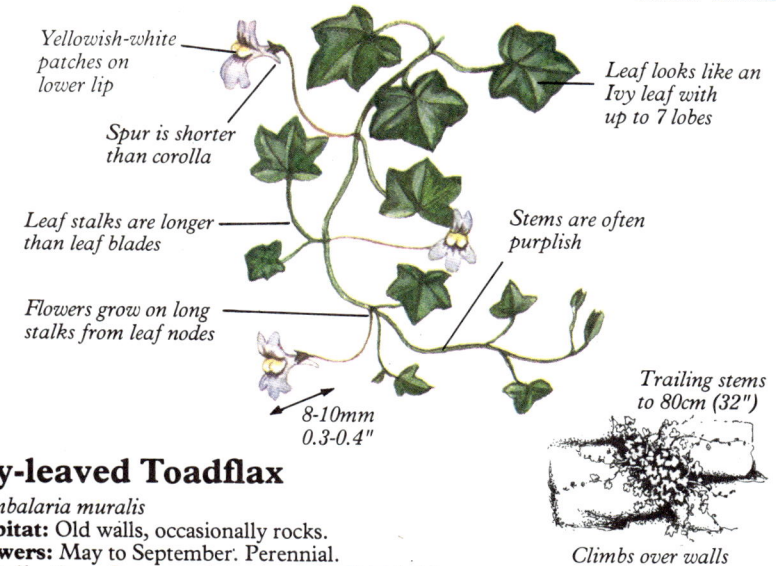

Yellowish-white patches on lower lip

Spur is shorter than corolla

Leaf stalks are longer than leaf blades

Flowers grow on long stalks from leaf nodes

Leaf looks like an Ivy leaf with up to 7 lobes

Stems are often purplish

8-10mm
0.3-0.4"

Trailing stems to 80cm (32")

Climbs over walls often forming clumps

Ivy-leaved Toadflax
Cymbalaria muralis
Habitat: Old walls, occasionally rocks.
Flowers: May to September. Perennial.
Distribution: Common throughout the British Isles.

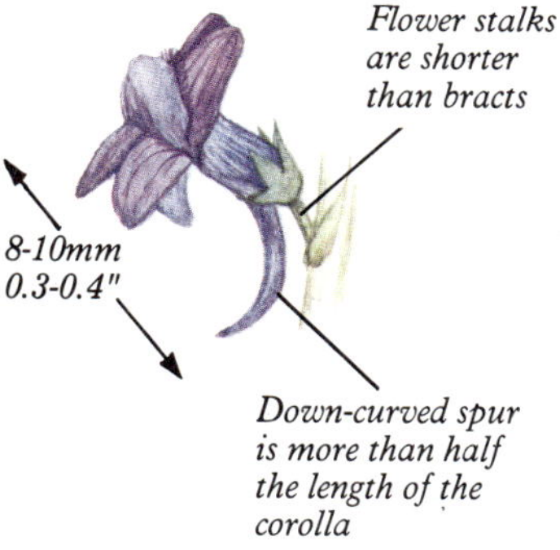

Flower stalks are shorter than bracts

8-10mm
0.3-0.4"

Down-curved spur is more than half the length of the corolla

Many flowers grow at ends of stems and branches

Hairless, grey-green plant

Long, narrow leaves

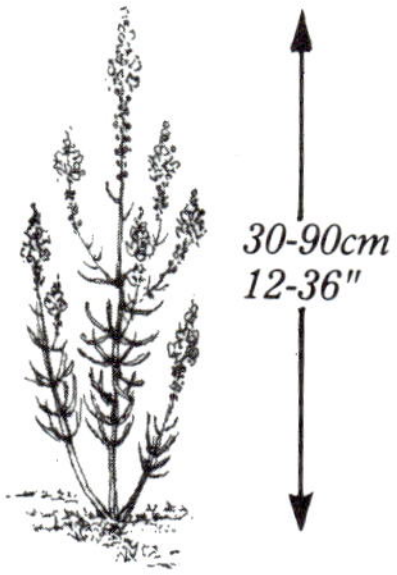

30-90cm
12-36"

Purple Toadflax
Linaria purpurea
Habitat: Waste ground, old walls, gardens.
Flowers: June to August. Perennial.
Distribution: Locally common throughout central and southern England; rare elsewhere.

Long, upright stems

PURPLE **PEA**

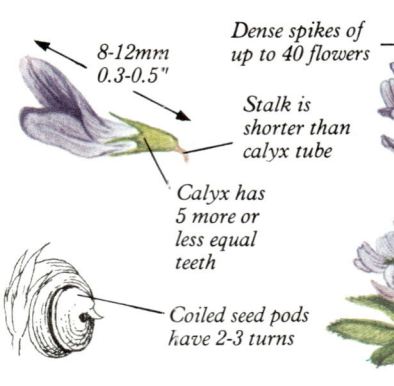

8-12mm
0.3-0.5"

Dense spikes of up to 40 flowers

Stalk is shorter than calyx tube

Calyx has 5 more or less equal teeth

Coiled seed pods have 2-3 turns

Narrow, pointed, toothed stipules

Hybrids formed with Sickle Medic can be many colours — black has been recorded

Leaves of 3 leaflets, each toothed at top: leaf shape is variable

30-90cm
12-36"

Plant is hairless and usually upright

Lucerne

Medicago sativa
Also called: Alfalfa.
Habitat: Waste ground, grassland.
Flowers: June to September. Perennial.
Distribution: Common in central and eastern England; scattered in Wales and Ireland; rare in Scotland.

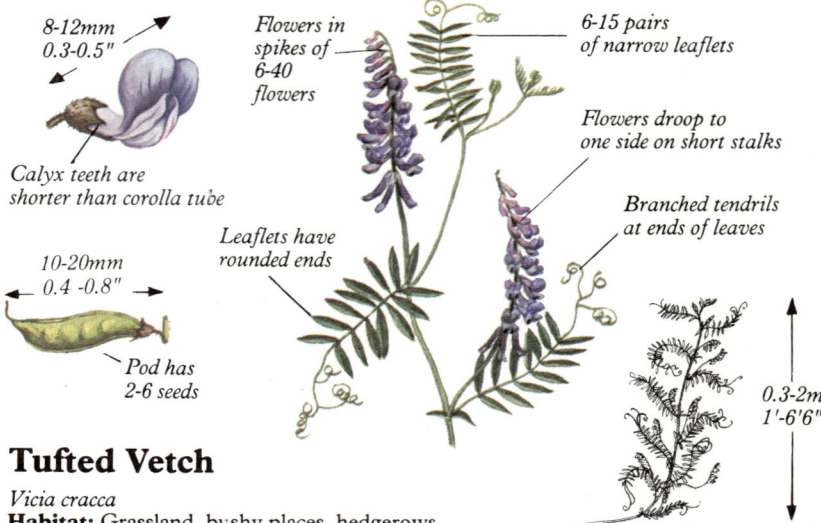

8-12mm
0.3-0.5"

Calyx teeth are shorter than corolla tube

10-20mm
0.4-0.8"

Pod has 2-6 seeds

Flowers in spikes of 6-40 flowers

Leaflets have rounded ends

6-15 pairs of narrow leaflets

Flowers droop to one side on short stalks

Branched tendrils at ends of leaves

0.3-2m
1'-6'6"

Climbs vegetation using its tendrils

Tufted Vetch

Vicia cracca
Habitat: Grassland, bushy places, hedgerows.
Flowers: June to August. Perennial.
Distribution: Common throughout the British Isles.

BLUE **4 PETALS**

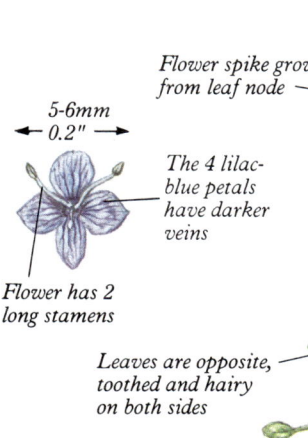

5-6mm
0.2"

Flower spike grows from leaf node

The 4 lilac-blue petals have darker veins

Flower has 2 long stamens

Leaves are opposite, toothed and hairy on both sides

Flower spike is long-stalked, conical and dense

Do not confuse with the many other *Speedwells* which usually have bluer flowers; the dense flower spike gives this species away.

Stems creep and root at intervals

10-30cm
4-12"

Common Speedwell
Veronica officinalis
Also called: Heath Speedwell.
Habitat: Grassland and open woods.
Flowers: May to August. Perennial.
Distribution: Common throughout the British Isles.

Plant forms large mats; stems often hidden in grass

Long, thin flower spikes grow in pairs from leaf nodes

The 2 stamens are white and long

4-9mm
0.2-0.4"

Petals have white bases

Plant is hairless

Do not confuse with *Water Speedwell* which has smaller pale blue flowers, or *Evergreen Alkanet* which is stiffly hairy.

Stems are upright, reddish, thick and hollow

Shiny leaves are fairly thick and fleshy

20-60cm
8-24"

Brooklime
Veronica beccabunga
Habitat: In and by ponds, streams, wet places.
Flowers: May to September. Perennial.
Distribution: Common throughout the British Isles.

Creeping, rooting base of stem may give large clumps

43

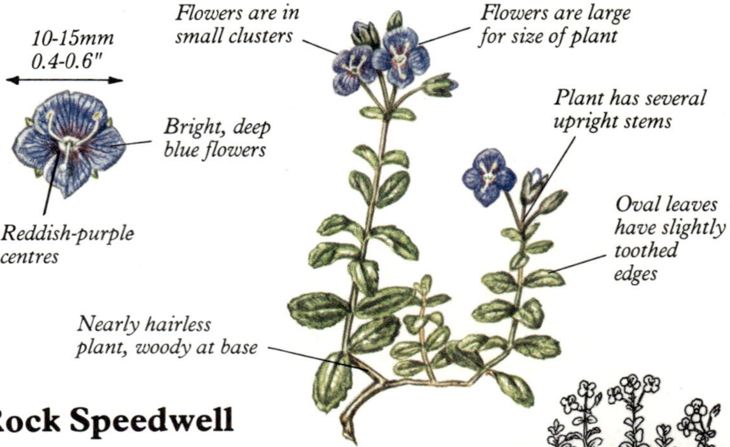

BLUE 4 PETALS/5 PETALS

10-15mm
0.4-0.6"

Flowers are in small clusters

Flowers are large for size of plant

Bright, deep blue flowers

Plant has several upright stems

Reddish-purple centres

Oval leaves have slightly toothed edges

Nearly hairless plant, woody at base

Rock Speedwell

Veronica fruticans
Also called: Shrubby Speedwell.
Habitat: Rocky mountain ledges and grassland.
Flowers: July to August. Perennial.
Distribution: Only in the central Scottish Highlands.

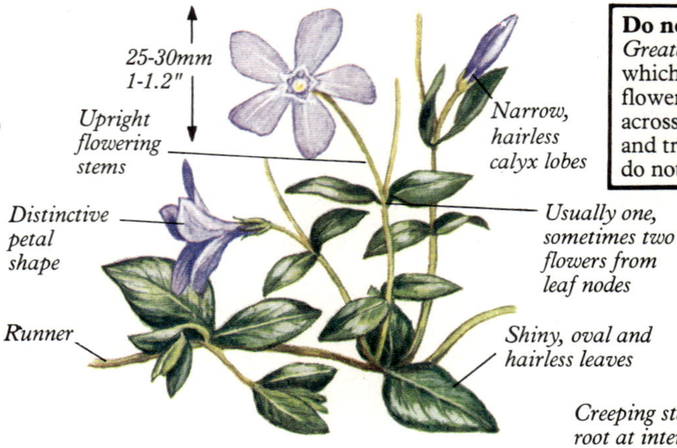

5-20cm
2-8"

Plant has the form of a small shrub

25-30mm
1-1.2"

Upright flowering stems

Narrow, hairless calyx lobes

Do not confuse with *Greater Periwinkle* which has larger flowers 40-50mm across, hairy calyces and trailing stems that do not root.

Distinctive petal shape

Usually one, sometimes two flowers from leaf nodes

Runner

Shiny, oval and hairless leaves

Creeping stems root at intervals

Lesser Periwinkle

Vinca minor
Habitat: Woods, hedgebanks, rockeries, gardens.
Flowers: March to May. Perennial.
Distribution: Local throughout the British Isles.

10-60cm
4-24"

Plant forms a leafy carpet

BLUE 5 PETALS

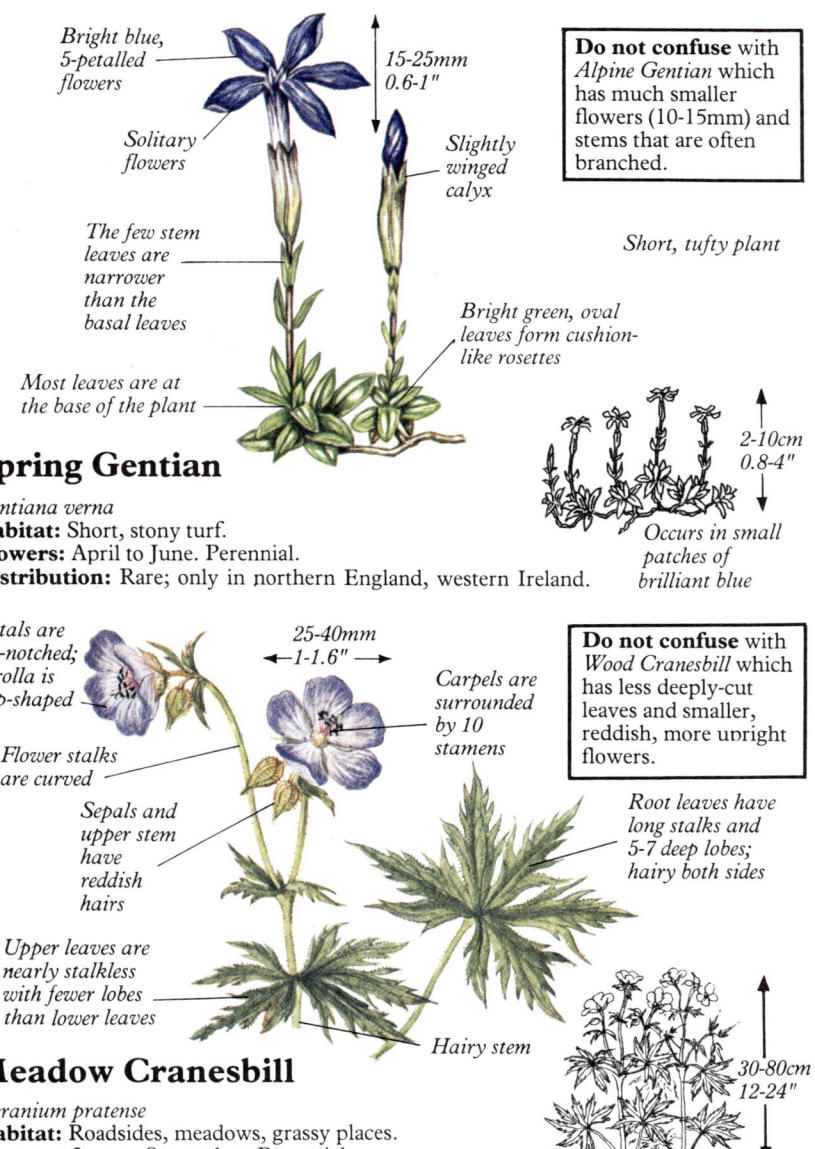

Bright blue, 5-petalled flowers

15-25mm 0.6-1"

Do not confuse with *Alpine Gentian* which has much smaller flowers (10-15mm) and stems that are often branched.

Solitary flowers

Slightly winged calyx

The few stem leaves are narrower than the basal leaves

Short, tufty plant

Bright green, oval leaves form cushion-like rosettes

Most leaves are at the base of the plant

2-10cm 0.8-4"

Spring Gentian
Gentiana verna
Habitat: Short, stony turf.
Flowers: April to June. Perennial.
Distribution: Rare; only in northern England, western Ireland.

Occurs in small patches of brilliant blue

Petals are un-notched; corolla is cup-shaped

25-40mm 1-1.6"

Carpels are surrounded by 10 stamens

Do not confuse with *Wood Cranesbill* which has less deeply-cut leaves and smaller, reddish, more upright flowers.

Flower stalks are curved

Sepals and upper stem have reddish hairs

Root leaves have long stalks and 5-7 deep lobes; hairy both sides

Upper leaves are nearly stalkless with fewer lobes than lower leaves

Hairy stem

Meadow Cranesbill
Geranium pratense
Habitat: Roadsides, meadows, grassy places.
Flowers: June to September. Perennial.
Distribution: Widespread but local throughout the British Isles except in Ireland and northern Scotland.

30-80cm 12-24"

Usually grows in clumps

45

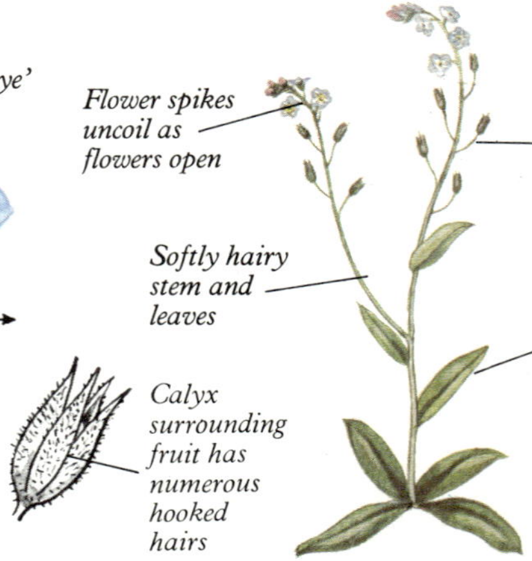

BLUE 5 PETALS

Bright yellow 'eye'

Flower spikes uncoil as flowers open

Fruit stalks are longer than calyx

4-5mm
0.2"

Softly hairy stem and leaves

Stem leaves are lance-shaped

Calyx surrounding fruit has numerous hooked hairs

7-30cm
3-12"

Common Forget-me-not

Myosotis arvensis
Also called: Field Forget-me-not, Scorpion Grass.
Habitat: Woods, hedgerows, wasteland, dunes.
Flowers: April to October. Annual or biennial.
Distribution: Common throughout the British Isles.

Basal leaves are stalked and form a rosette

Corolla is first reddish purple, maturing to bright blue

Narrow, pointed leaves are dark green above, light green below

12-15mm
0.5-0.6"

Each lobe of corolla has darker central base

Dense clusters of flowers elongate after flowering

10-60cm
4-24"

Stem and leaves are hairy

Blue Gromwell

Buglossoides purpurocaerulea
Also called: Purple Gromwell.
Habitat: Wood edges, hedgebanks.
Flowers: May to June. Perennial.
Distribution: Rare; only in western England and Wales.

Creeping, woody stems have flowering and non-flowering shoots

BLUE **5 PETALS**

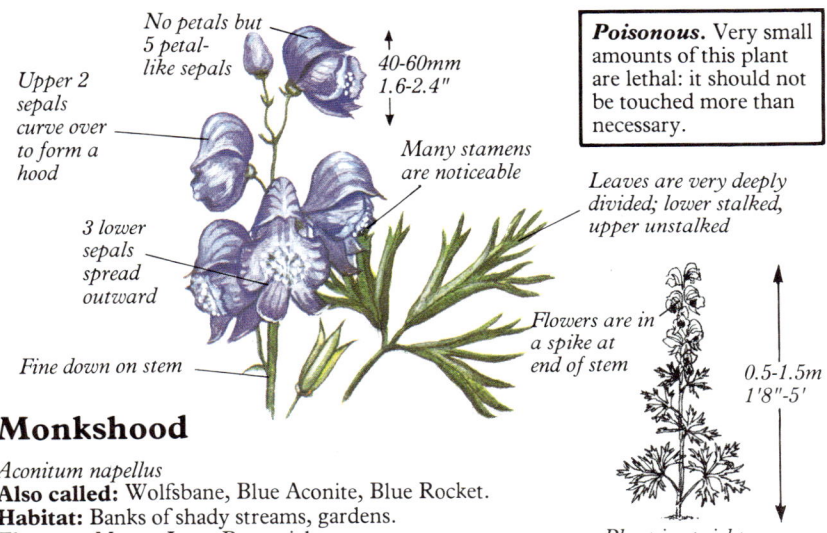

No petals but 5 petal-like sepals

Upper 2 sepals curve over to form a hood

40-60mm 1.6-2.4"

Poisonous. Very small amounts of this plant are lethal: it should not be touched more than necessary.

Many stamens are noticeable

Leaves are very deeply divided; lower stalked, upper unstalked

3 lower sepals spread outward

Flowers are in a spike at end of stem

Fine down on stem

0.5-1.5m 1'8"-5'

Monkshood

Aconitum napellus
Also called: Wolfsbane, Blue Aconite, Blue Rocket.
Habitat: Banks of shady streams, gardens.
Flowers: May to June. Perennial.
Distribution: Very local in south-west England and Wales.

Plant is upright, usually unbranched

20-30mm 0.8-1.2"

Flowers are in loose spikes

Stem and leaves have rough, bristly hairs

5 calyx teeth are narrow, pointed and stiffly hairy

Lower leaves are stalked and oval, with wavy edges

Leaf stalk has blade running down it like a spine

Black stamens form a prominent central column

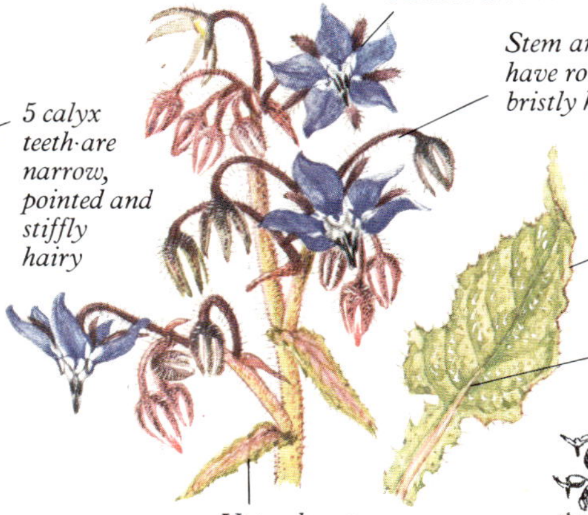

Upper leaves are stalkless

20-60cm 8-24"

Borage

Borago officinalis
Habitat: Waste ground, roadsides, especially near habitation.
Flowers: May to September. Annual.
Distribution: Scattered throughout the British Isles.

Plant is stout, upright and spreading

BLUE 6+ PETALS/COMPOSITE

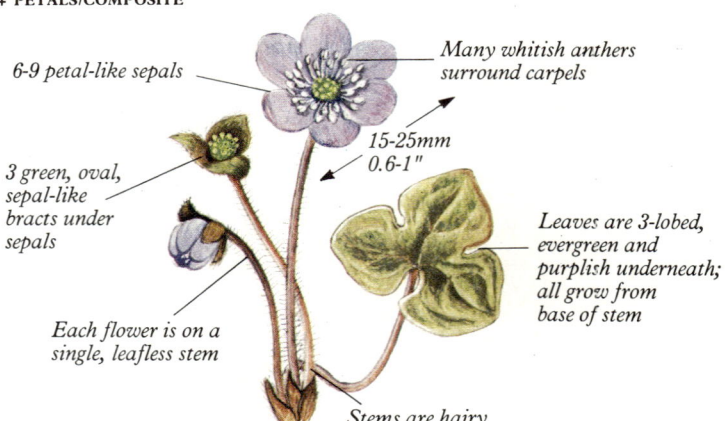

Hepatica

Hepatica nobilis
Habitat: Open woodlands.
Flowers: March to April. Perennial.
Distribution: Found only as a garden plant in the British Isles; grows wild on the Continent.

Usually grows in small clumps

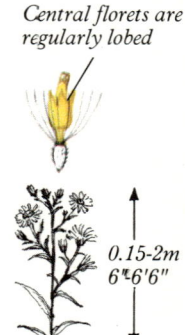

Michaelmas Daisy

Aster novi-belgii
Habitat: Waste ground, roadsides, gardens.
Flowers: August to November. Perennial.
Distribution: Scattered throughout the British Isles.

BLUE **COMPOSITE**

Sea Holly
Eryngium maritimum
Habitat: Sandy and shingly shores.
Flowers: June to September. Perennial.
Distribution: Fairly common on all coasts.

Devil's Bit Scabious
Succisa pratensis
Habitat: Wet grassy areas.
Flowers: June to October. Perennial.
Distribution: Common throughout the British Isles.

BLUE **COMPOSITE**

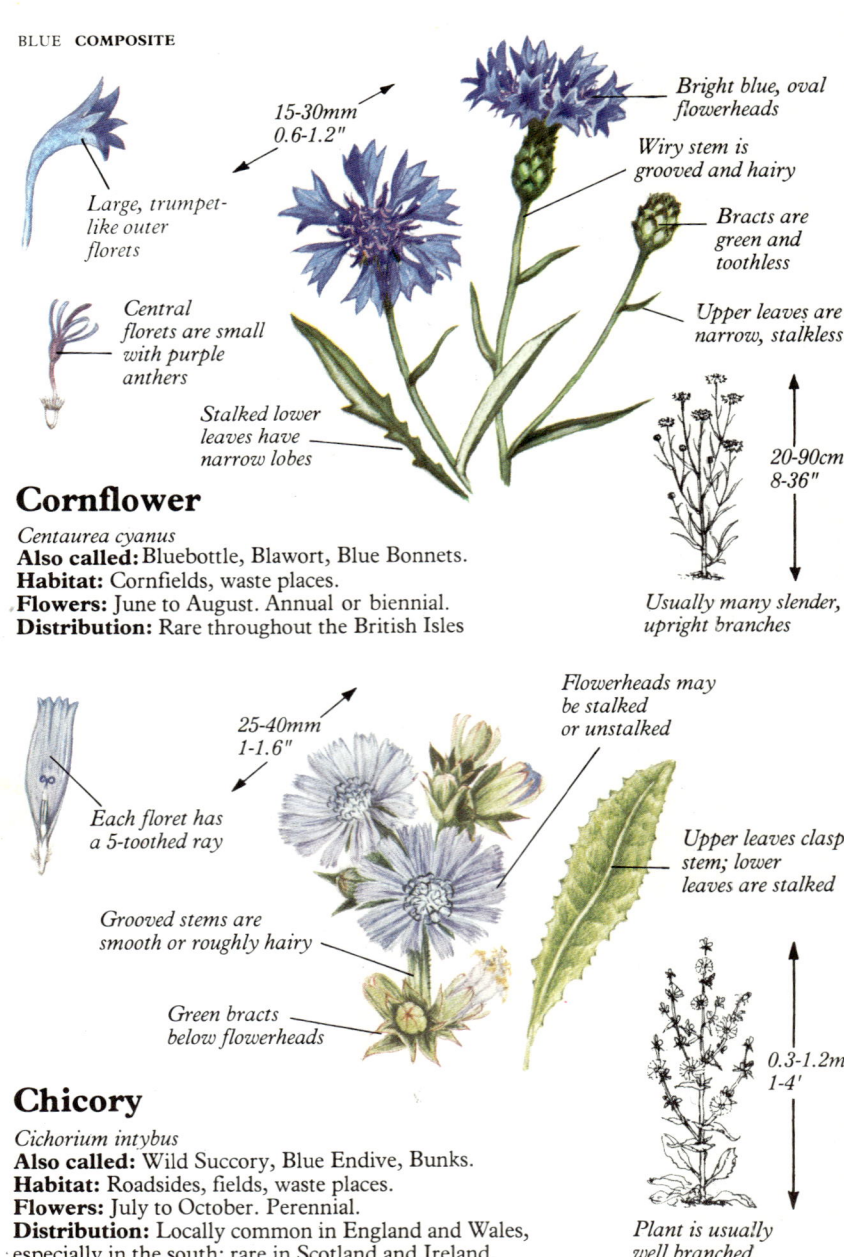

Bright blue, oval flowerheads

15-30mm 0.6-1.2"

Wiry stem is grooved and hairy

Large, trumpet-like outer florets

Bracts are green and toothless

Central florets are small with purple anthers

Upper leaves are narrow, stalkless

Stalked lower leaves have narrow lobes

20-90cm 8-36"

Cornflower

Centaurea cyanus
Also called: Bluebottle, Blawort, Blue Bonnets.
Habitat: Cornfields, waste places.
Flowers: June to August. Annual or biennial.
Distribution: Rare throughout the British Isles

Usually many slender, upright branches

Flowerheads may be stalked or unstalked

25-40mm 1-1.6"

Each floret has a 5-toothed ray

Upper leaves clasp stem; lower leaves are stalked

Grooved stems are smooth or roughly hairy

Green bracts below flowerheads

Chicory

Cichorium intybus
Also called: Wild Succory, Blue Endive, Bunks.
Habitat: Roadsides, fields, waste places.
Flowers: July to October. Perennial.
Distribution: Locally common in England and Wales, especially in the south; rare in Scotland and Ireland.

0.3-1.2m 1-4'

Plant is usually well branched

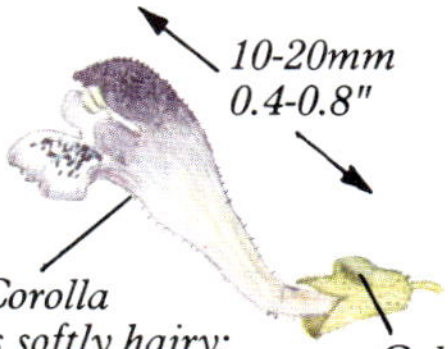

BLUE **LIPPED**

Plant is short, creeping, often downy

10-20mm 0.4-0.8"

Corolla is softly hairy; much longer than calyx

Calyx has small pouch on top

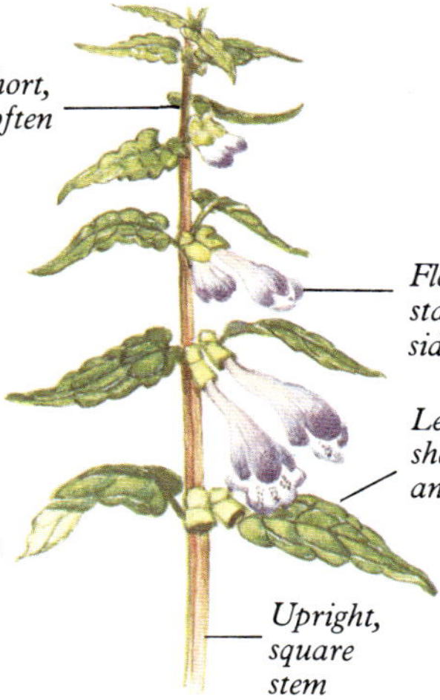

Do not confuse with *Lesser Skullcap* which has smaller (6-10mm) pinkish-purple flowers.

Flowers are in pairs on short stalks and usually face to one side of stem

Leaves are opposite with shallow, blunt teeth and short stalks

Upright, square stem

10-50cm 4-20"

Common Skullcap

Scutellaria galericulata
Habitat: Wet, grassy areas, usually by fresh water.
Flowers: June to September. Perennial.
Distribution: Common throughout the British Isles.

Plant often covers large patches

Flowers are in whorls

4 stamens and style project

Short upper lip

Upper leaves are shorter than flowers

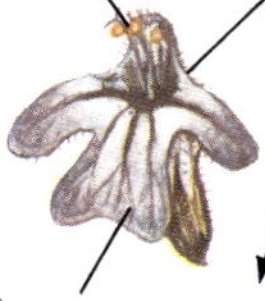

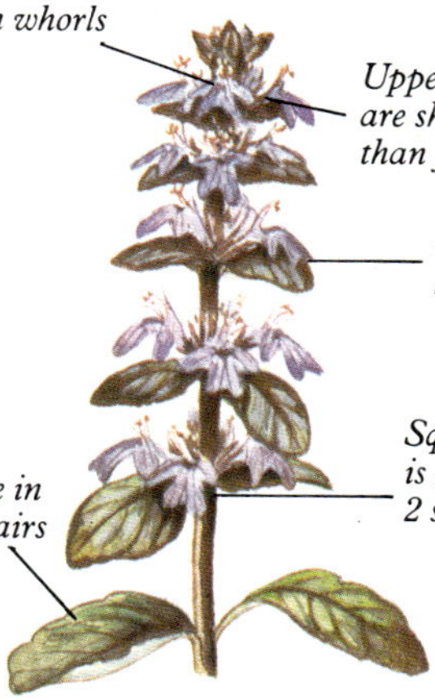

Do not confuse with other *Bugles* which have no runners, or *Ground Ivy* (p52).

Glossy leaves have hairy edges

7-9mm 0.3"

Large lower lip

Leaves are in opposite pairs and often purplish

Square stem is hairy on 2 sides

10-30cm 4-12"

Common Bugle

Ajuga reptans
Habitat: Moist soils, meadows, banks, open woods.
Flowers: May to July. Perennial.
Distribution: Common throughout the British Isles.

Creeping, rooting runners

51

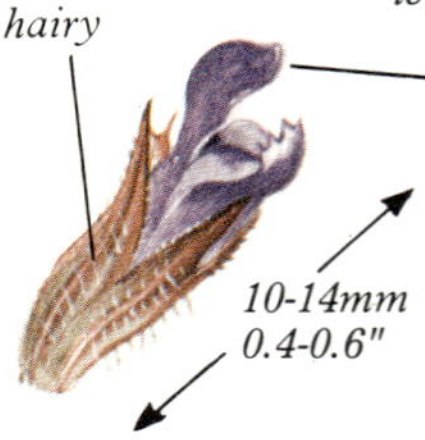

BLUE **LIPPED**

Calyx has 2 lips that are toothed and hairy

Bracts and calyces have long white hairs

Do not confuse with *Cut-leaved Self Heal* which has deeply-cut leaves, or *Large-flowered Self Heal* which has flowers 20-25mm long.

Upper lip is longer than lower

Stem is square and slightly hairy

10-14mm 0.4-0.6"

Flowers may also be pink or white

Flowers squashed together in dense, squarish spikes at end of stem

Leaves are oval, usually stalked, sometimes shallowly toothed

5-30cm 2-12"

Self Heal

Prunella vulgaris
Habitat: Grassland, open woodland, waste places.
Flowers: June to September. Perennial.
Distribution: Common throughout the British Isles.

Creeping plant with many flowering stems

Forked style protrudes from under upper lip

Leaves are opposite with rounded teeth

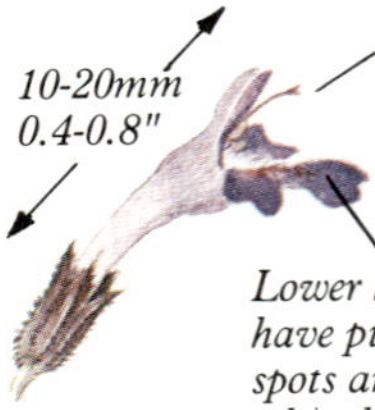

Do not confuse with *Common Skullcap* (p51) which has longer, paler flowers, or *Common Bugle* (p51).

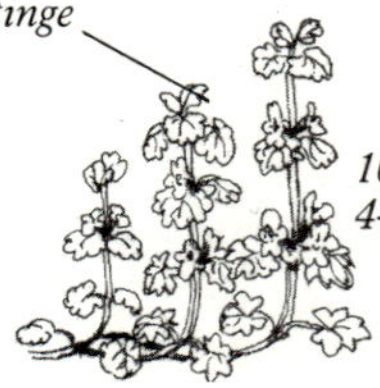

10-20mm 0.4-0.8"

Lower lips have purple spots and white hairs inside

Flowers are in whorls of 2-6 at leaf nodes

Plant is low, creeping, often with purplish tinge

Stem is square and softly hairy

Flowering stems are upright

10-60cm 4-24"

Ground Ivy

Glechoma hederacea
Habitat: Woodland, roadsides, grassy areas.
Flowers: March to June. Perennial.
Distribution: Common throughout the British Isles.

Plant forms large clumps

BLUE LIPPED/TUBULAR OR BELL

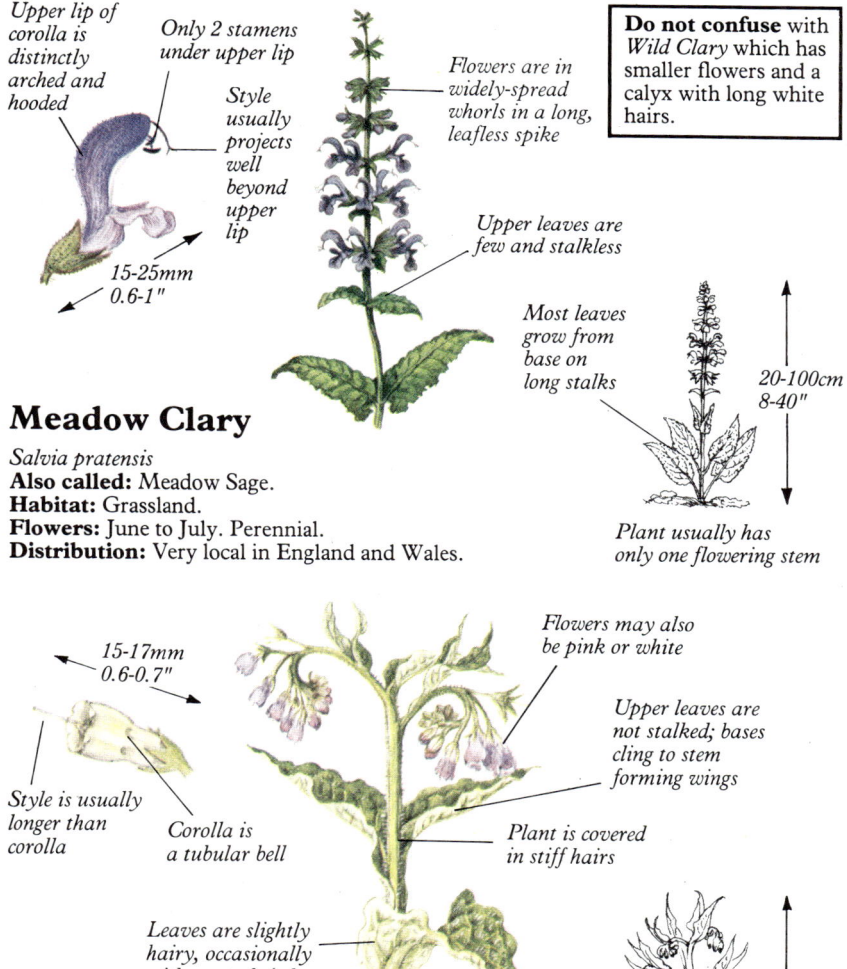

Upper lip of corolla is distinctly arched and hooded

Only 2 stamens under upper lip

Style usually projects well beyond upper lip

15-25mm
0.6-1"

Flowers are in widely-spread whorls in a long, leafless spike

Do not confuse with *Wild Clary* which has smaller flowers and a calyx with long white hairs.

Upper leaves are few and stalkless

Most leaves grow from base on long stalks

20-100cm
8-40"

Meadow Clary

Salvia pratensis
Also called: Meadow Sage.
Habitat: Grassland.
Flowers: June to July. Perennial.
Distribution: Very local in England and Wales.

Plant usually has only one flowering stem

15-17mm
0.6-0.7"

Flowers may also be pink or white

Upper leaves are not stalked; bases cling to stem forming wings

Style is usually longer than corolla

Corolla is a tubular bell

Plant is covered in stiff hairs

Leaves are slightly hairy, occasionally with warty bristles

Common Comfrey

Symphytum officinale
Habitat: Damp places, especially by running water.
Flowers: May to July. Perennial.
Distribution: Common throughout the British Isles.

0.3-1.2m
1-4'

Lower leaves are stalked

BLUE TUBULAR OR BELL

4 stamens protrude

Sharp hairs

Flowers are in dense spikes; pink at first, turning purplish blue with age

15-20mm
0.6-0.8"

Speckled stem

Pink buds

Bristly leaves

Feathery sepals hide fruit

Viper's Bugloss

Echium vulgare
Habitat: Grassy areas.
Flowers: June to September. Biennial.
Distribution: Locally common in southern England and Wales; rare in Scotland and Ireland.

30-90cm
12-36"

Stalked rosette leaves

Flowers droop from one side of stem

Fragrant flowers can be white or pink

Bracts are bluish and grow in pairs

Short stalks

15-20mm
0.6-0.8"

Keeled, glossy, strap-like leaves grow from base

3 long and 3 short stamens with cream anthers

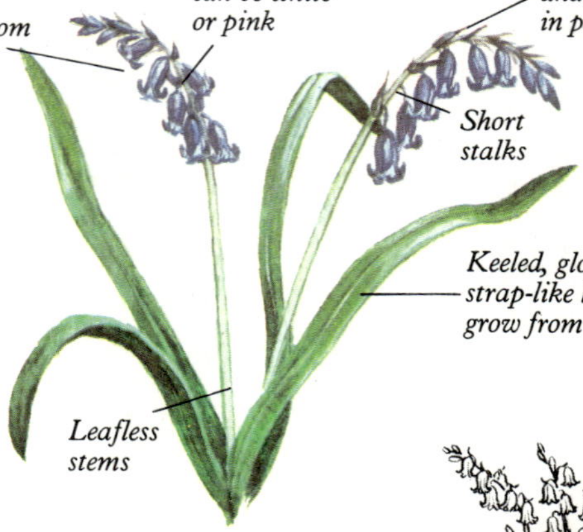

Leafless stems

Bluebell

Hyacinthoides non-scripta
Also called: Wild Hyacinth, Blue Bottle, Crow Flower.
Habitat: Woods, scrub, hedgerows, cliffs.
Flowers: April to June. Perennial.
Distribution: Common throughout the British Isles.

20-50cm
8-40"

Often covers large patches

BLUE **TUBULAR OR BELL**

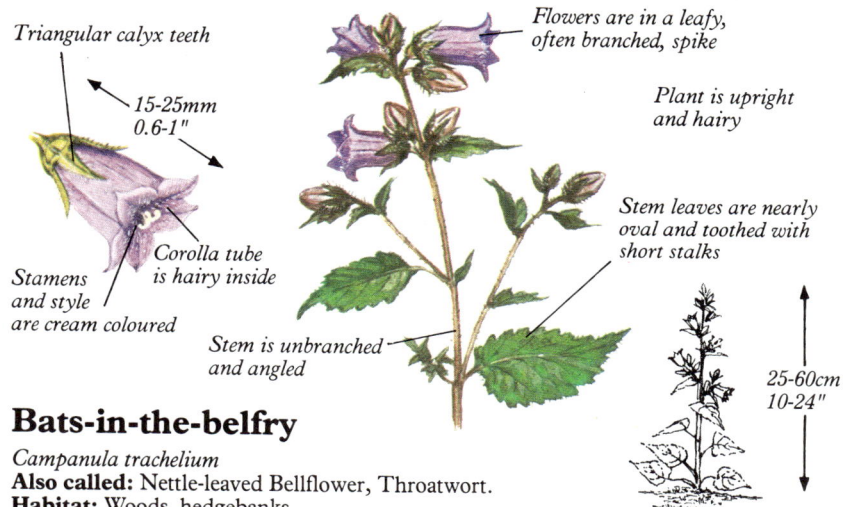

Bats-in-the-belfry
Campanula trachelium
Also called: Nettle-leaved Bellflower, Throatwort.
Habitat: Woods, hedgebanks.
Flowers: July to September. Perennial.
Distribution: Local throughout the British Isles.

Do not confuse with other *Bellflowers* which all have stouter stems, less delicate flowers and usually toothed leaves.

Harebell
Campanula rotundifolia
Also called: Bluebell, Lady's Thimble, Devil's Bell.
Habitat: Dry, grassy places.
Flowers: July to September. Perennial.
Distribution: Locally common throughout the British Isles.

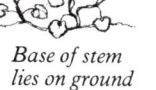

Base of stem lies on ground

BLUE **SPURRED**

30-50mm
1.2-2"

Flowers are on long stems

Each petal has a long, sharp, curved spur

Flowers are sometimes white or reddish

Sepals are oval and blue

Plant is **poisonous**

Upper leaves have short stalks

Stalkless bracts have 3 narrow lobes

Leaf has 3 leaflets each with 3 parts

Stem is hairless or softly hairy

0.3-1m
1'-3'3"

Columbine

Aquilegia vulgaris
Habitat: Open woods, scrubland, damp places.
Flowers: May to June. Perennial.
Distribution: Local throughout the British Isles.

Basal leaves are on long stalks

30-40mm
1.2-1.6"

Spur is longer than sepals

Flowers are on stalks in dense spikes

Do not confuse with *Forking Larkspur* which has flower stalks longer than bracts, or *Eastern Larkspur* which has flower stalks shorter than bracts.

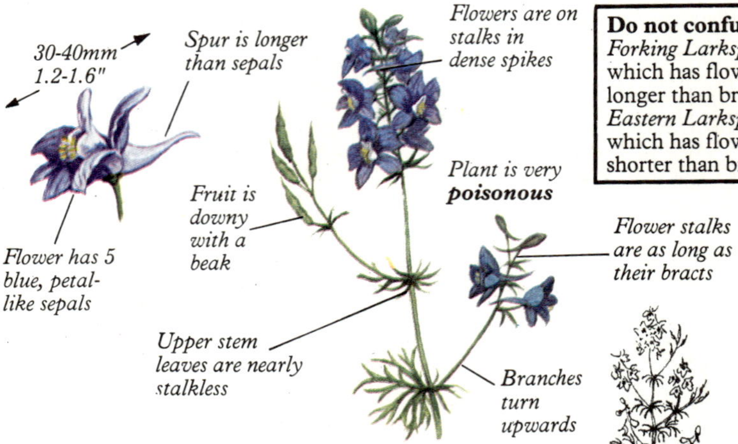

Fruit is downy with a beak

Plant is very **poisonous**

Flower has 5 blue, petal-like sepals

Flower stalks are as long as their bracts

Upper stem leaves are nearly stalkless

Branches turn upwards

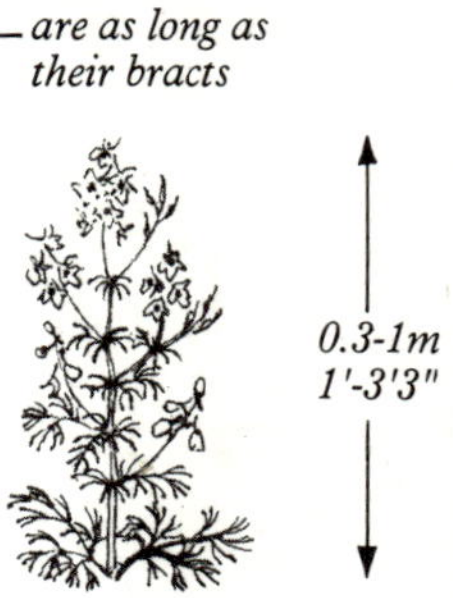

0.3-1m
1'-3'3"

Larkspur

Consolida ambigua
Habitat: Arable ground, waste places.
Flowers: June to July. Annual.
Distribution: Scattered throughout the British Isles.

Plant is upright, branched and softly hairy

BLUE **SPURRED/PEA**

Spur is blunt, paler than corolla, notched and often turned upwards

14-22mm 0.6-0.9"

Do not confuse with *Wood Dog Violet* which has a straight spur, darker than the corolla, or *Sweet Violet* which is scented.

Upper petals are curved back

Narrow, pointed sepals

Leaves are heart-shaped

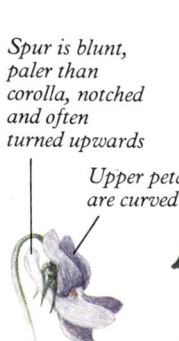

Plant is hairless or slightly downy

Well-toothed stipules

Common Dog Violet

Viola riviniana
Habitat: Woods, hedges, paths, banks.
Flowers: April to June. Perennial.
Distribution: Common throughout the British Isles.

5-30cm
2-12"

Often grows in large clumps

Flowers can be purple or dirty white

Leaflets have squared ends

Do not confuse with *Smooth Tare* which has 4-seeded pods that are hairless

4-5mm 0.2"

Tiny flowers are in spikes of up to 9 flowers

4-10 pairs of leaflets and branched tendrils

Calyx teeth are longer than corolla tube

Hairy pod usually has 2 seeds

Plant is more or less hairless

Thin stems

Hairy Tare

Vicia hirsuta
Habitat: Grassy places, cornfields.
Flowers: May to August. Annual.
Distribution: Common throughout much of the British Isles; rarer in Ireland and north-western Scotland.

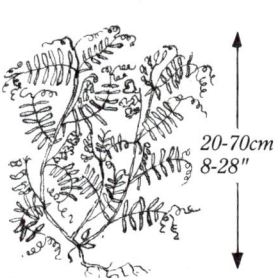

20-70cm
8-28"

Sprawling, untidy plant

WHITE 0-3 PETALS

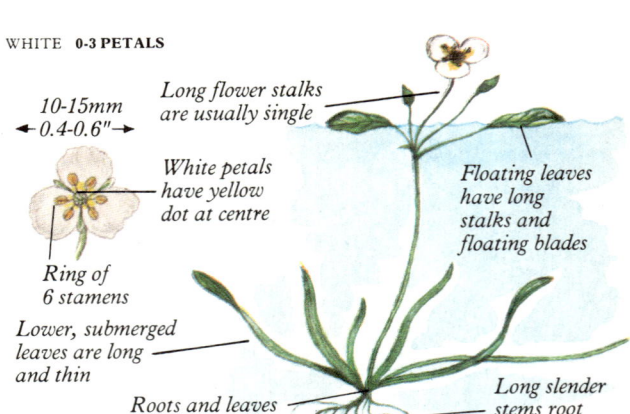

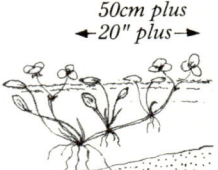

Leaves and flower stalks are visible above the surface

Floating Water Plantain

Luronium natans
Habitat: Lakes, canals, slow water.
Flowers: May to August. Perennial.
Distribution: Rare; mainly in Wales and north-west England and mostly absent elsewhere.

Grows very long in still water

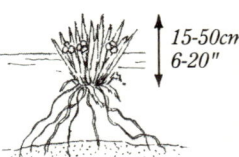

Flowers and leaf tips are visible above water

Water Soldier

Stratiotes aloides
Habitat: Ponds, ditches, canals.
Flowers: June to August. Perennial.
Distribution: Mainly in eastern England; absent from northern Scotland; scattered elsewhere.

Plant rises to surface only for flowering

WHITE 0-3 PETALS/4 PETALS

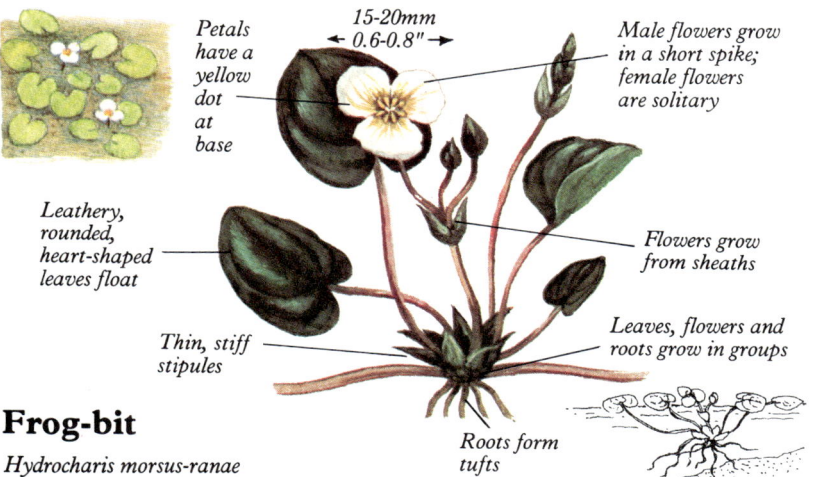

Frog-bit

Hydrocharis morsus-ranae
Habitat: Ponds, canals, ditches.
Flowers: July to August. Perennial.
Distribution: Scattered throughout England, Wales and Ireland; absent from Scotland.

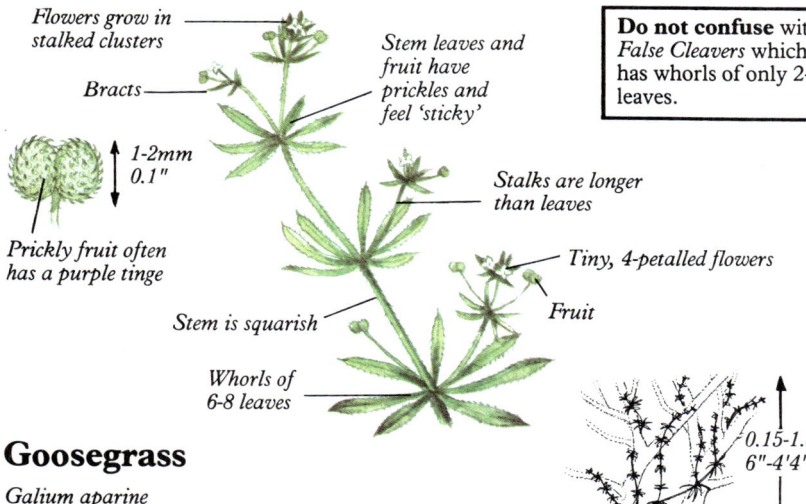

Goosegrass

Galium aparine
Also called: Cleavers, Hedgeheriff, Hayriff.
Habitat: Hedgebanks, woods, open ground.
Flowers: May to August. Annual.
Distribution: Common throughout the British Isles.

59

WHITE **4 PETALS**

Small cluster of flowers becomes a spike of fruits

5-8mm 0.2-0.3"

Fruits are long, thin, upright and squarish

4 petals arranged in a cross

All leaves are wavy, glossy and crinkled

Heart-shaped basal leaves have long stalks

Stem leaves are more triangular with short stalks

Toothed edges

Smells of garlic when crushed

0.2-1.2m 8"-4'

Garlic Mustard

Alliaria petiolata
Also called: Hedge Garlic, Jack-by-the-hedge.
Habitat: Hedges, waysides, wood edges.
Flowers: April to June. Biennial.
Distribution: Common in England, Wales and southern Scotland; local in Ireland; absent from the far north.

Often occurs in large patches

Short, crowded spikes of flowers

6-8mm 0.2-0.3"

Stem is short, slightly downy and branched

Outer petals are twice as long as inner petals

Mauve flowers also occur

Leaves are toothed and scattered along stem

10-30cm 4-12"

Wild Candytuft

Iberis amara
Habitat: Hillsides, fields, wasteground.
Flowers: May to September. Annual.
Distribution: Local in southern England only.

Well branched; size varies greatly

WHITE 4 PETALS

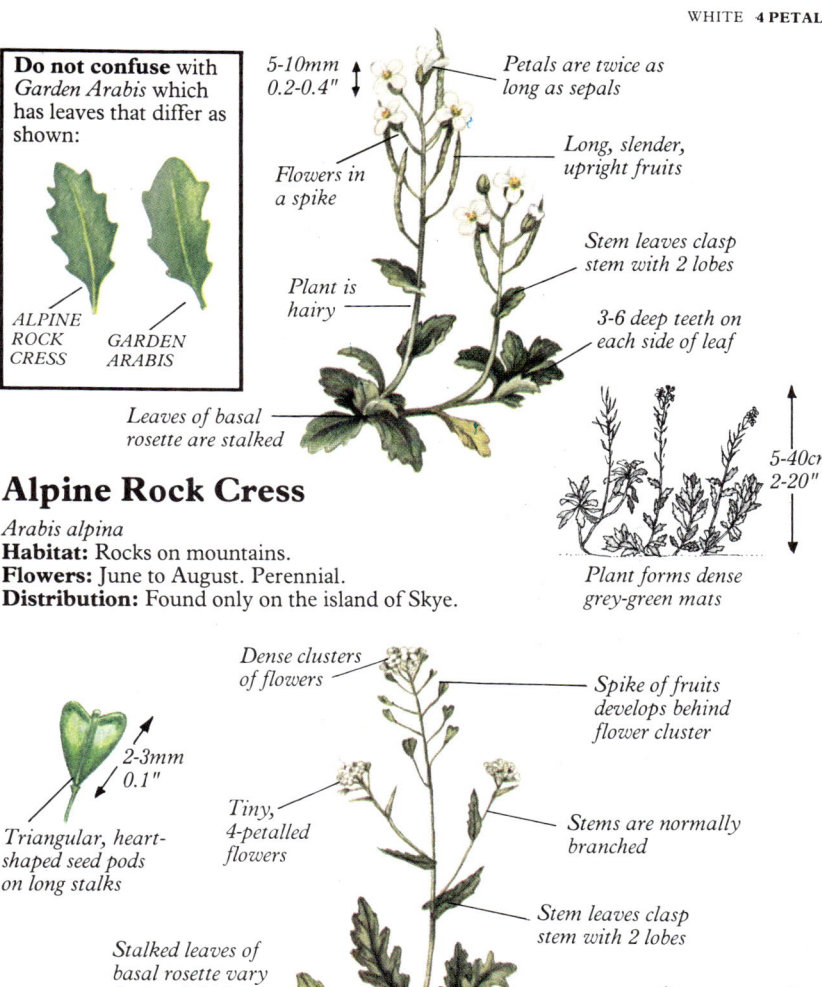

Alpine Rock Cress

Arabis alpina
Habitat: Rocks on mountains.
Flowers: June to August. Perennial.
Distribution: Found only on the island of Skye.

Shepherd's Purse

Capsella bursa-pastoris
Habitat: Waysides, waste places, cultivated land.
Flowers: All year. Annual or biennial.
Distribution: Common throughout the British Isles.

61

WHITE 5 PETALS

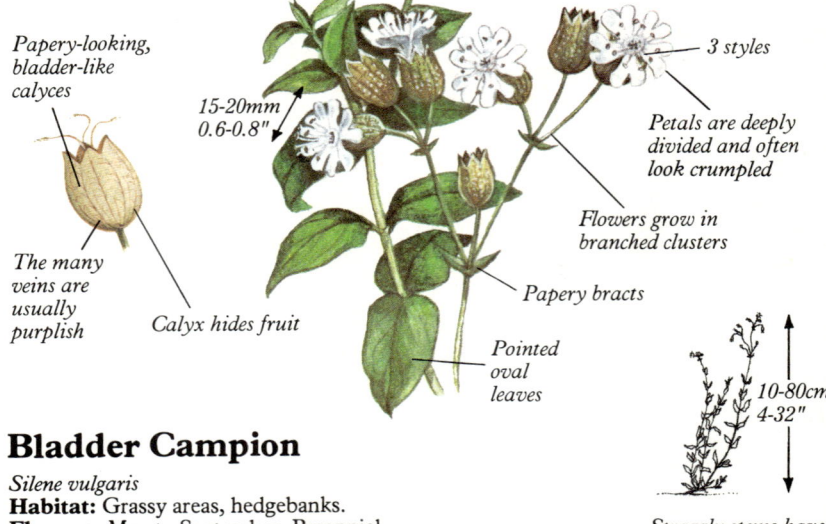

Bladder Campion
Silene vulgaris
Habitat: Grassy areas, hedgebanks.
Flowers: May to September. Perennial.
Distribution: Common throughout the British Isles.

White Campion
Silene alba
Habitat: Waysides, hedgebanks, waste ground.
Flowers: May to September. Annual or perennial.
Distribution: Common throughout the British Isles.

WHITE 5 PETALS

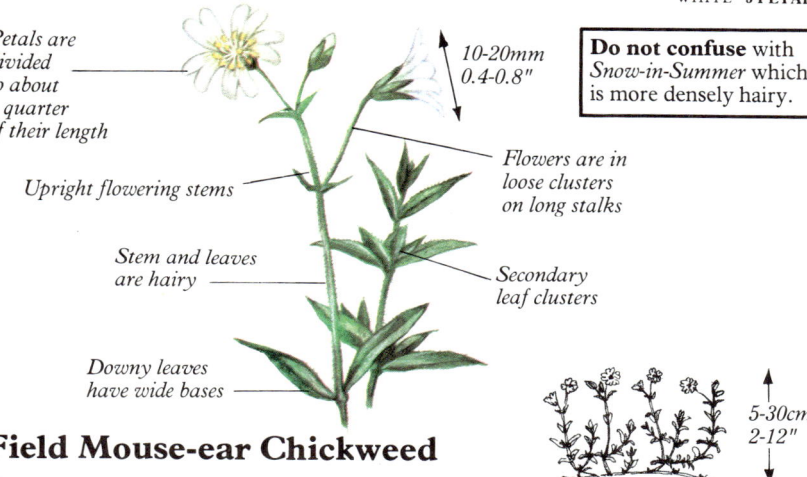

Petals are divided to about a quarter of their length

10-20mm
0.4-0.8"

Do not confuse with Snow-in-Summer which is more densely hairy.

Upright flowering stems

Flowers are in loose clusters on long stalks

Stem and leaves are hairy

Secondary leaf clusters

Downy leaves have wide bases

Field Mouse-ear Chickweed

Cerastium arvense
Habitat: Dry banks, fields, grassy places.
Flowers: April to August. Perennial.
Distribution: Locally common throughout the British Isles, especially in eastern England and Scotland.

5-30cm
2-12"

Rooting and non-flowering stems run along the ground – often hidden in grass

10 stamens around 3 styles

20-30mm
0.8-1.2"

Do not confuse with Lesser Stitchwort which has petals that are split almost to the base and are as long as sepals.

Plant is hairless

Flowers are on long stalks in loose clusters

LESSER   GREATER

Leaves are in opposite pairs and are narrowly pointed with rough edges

Large petals are split to about halfway and are longer than sepals

Greater Stitchwort

Stellaria holostea
Also called: Adder's Meat, Satin Flower, Shirt Buttons.
Habitat: Woods, hedgerows, roadsides.
Flowers: April to June. Perennial.
Distribution: Common throughout the British Isles.

10-60cm
4-24"

Plant also has short, non-flowering stems

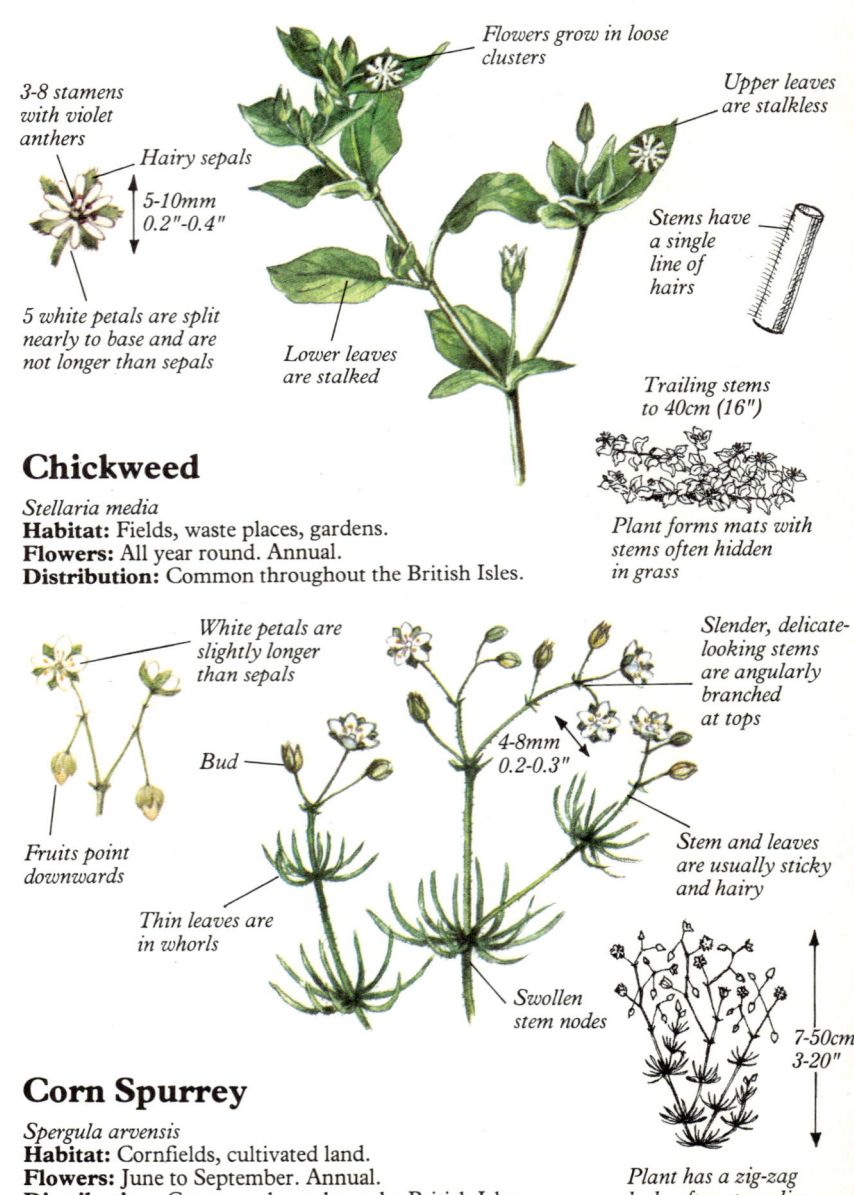

Chickweed

Stellaria media
Habitat: Fields, waste places, gardens.
Flowers: All year round. Annual.
Distribution: Common throughout the British Isles.

Corn Spurrey

Spergula arvensis
Habitat: Cornfields, cultivated land.
Flowers: June to September. Annual.
Distribution: Common throughout the British Isles.

WHITE **5 PETALS**

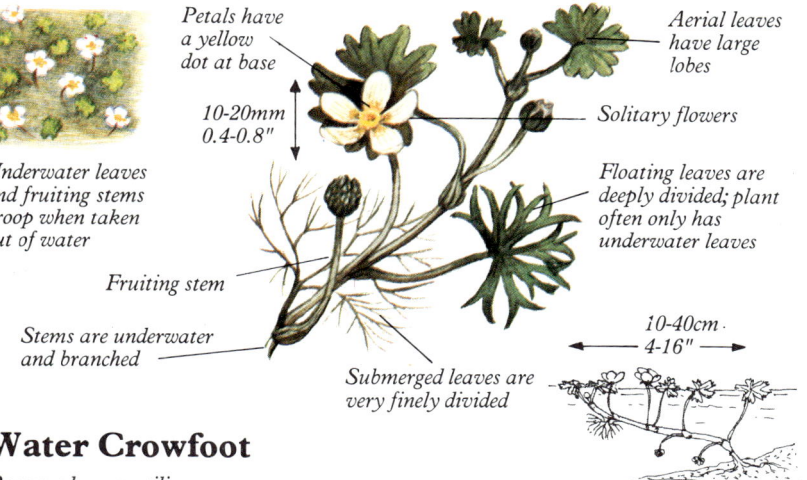

Petals have a yellow dot at base
10-20mm
0.4-0.8"

Aerial leaves have large lobes

Solitary flowers

Underwater leaves and fruiting stems droop when taken out of water

Floating leaves are deeply divided; plant often only has underwater leaves

Fruiting stem

Stems are underwater and branched

Submerged leaves are very finely divided

10-40cm
4-16"

Water Crowfoot

Ranunculus aquatilis
Habitat: Ditches, still and running water.
Flowers: April to September. Annual or perennial.
Distribution: Common throughout the British Isles.

Plant has many stems; flowers often cover surface

Thorns point backwards along stem

Long, toothed stipules

Leaves have 5-7 toothed leaflets

Many stamens

Sepals always drop before fruit is ripe

Fruit ('rose-hip') is oval, smooth and red

Flowers are stalked and may also be pink

35-50mm
1.4-2"

Lobed sepals

1-3m
3'3"-9'9"

Dog Rose

Rosa canina
Habitat: Hedges, woodlands, scrub.
Flowers: June to July. Perennial.
Distribution: Common throughout the British Isles though becoming rarer northwards in Scotland.

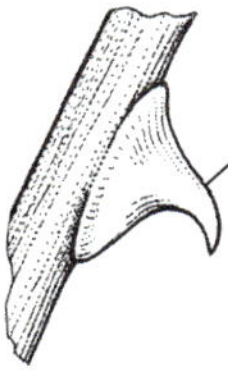

A vigorously scrambling plant

65

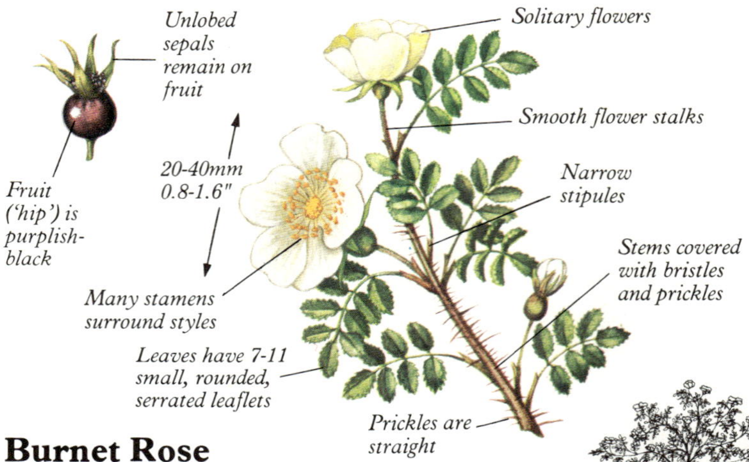

WHITE 5 PETALS

Solitary flowers

Unlobed sepals remain on fruit

Smooth flower stalks

20-40mm 0.8-1.6"

Narrow stipules

Fruit ('hip') is purplish-black

Stems covered with bristles and prickles

Many stamens surround styles

Leaves have 7-11 small, rounded, serrated leaflets

Prickles are straight

Burnet Rose

Rosa pimpinellifolia
Habitat: Hedges, dunes, heaths, by the sea.
Flowers: May to July. Perennial.
Distribution: Locally common throughout the British Isles.

10-50cm 4-20"

Forms large patches by spreading suckers

Leaves have 3-5 leaflets, often prickly underneath

Petals are white or occasionally pinkish

Stems may arch high or low, intertwine with fences or bushes, or form a tangled carpet

Fruit has many fleshy segments; ripens to black

Stems have sharp thorns and often bristles and hairs

Woody, usually angular stems

Blackberry

Rubus fruticosus
Also called: Bramble, Brier, Country Lawyers.
Habitat: Woods, scrub, hedges, open ground.
Flowers: May to November. Perennial.
Distribution: Common throughout the British Isles.

1-4m 3-10'

Arching stems root at tips

WHITE 5 PETALS

10-18mm
0.4-0.7"

Leaves have 3 leaflets

Hairy sepals

Many stamens

Petals overlap

Bright green leaflets are slightly hairy above

Leaves are pale with silky hairs beneath

Hairy flower and leaf stems

Fruit is smaller than garden strawberry

Do not confuse with *Barren Strawberry* which has distinct gaps between the notched petals.

BARREN STRAWBERRY

Short, softly hairy plant

5-30cm
2-12"

Long runners form fresh plants at rooting nodes; covers large areas

Wild Strawberry

Fragaria vesca
Habitat: Woods, scrub, disturbed ground.
Flowers: April to July. Perennial.
Distribution: Common throughout the British Isles.

Leaves fold at night and in bad weather

Leaf lobes are notched at tip

10-16mm
0.4-0.6"

Solitary flowers are on long leafless stalks

Yellow-green leaves have 3 lobes and long stalks

10 stamens

The 5 petals have lilac veins

Wood Sorrel

Oxalis acetosella
Habitat: Woods and hedgebanks.
Flowers: April to May. Perennial.
Distribution: Common throughout the British Isles.

5-15cm
2-6"

Plant may be solitary or in small groups

WHITE 5 PETALS

10-20mm
0.4-0.8"

Female flowers are in nearly stalkless clusters

Petals are very veined

Leaf and flower stalks, tendrils and branches all grow from the same point

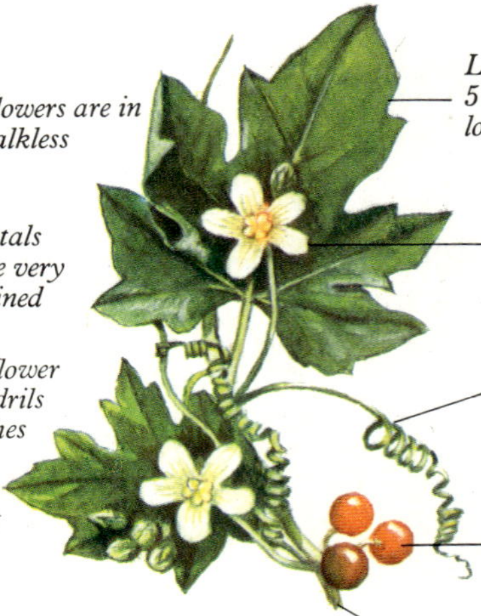

Leaves usually have 5 toothed, wavy-edged lobes

Male flowers grow in stalked spikes

Plant climbs by coiled tendrils

Berries ripen through yellow to red: **poisonous**

Hairy, brittle stems grow to 4m/13'

White Bryony

Bryonia dioica
Also called: Red Bryony, Mandrake, Wild Vine.
Habitat: Climbs in hedgerows and scrub.
Flowers: May to September. Perennial.
Distribution: Locally common in England; rare in Wales; absent from most of Scotland and Ireland.

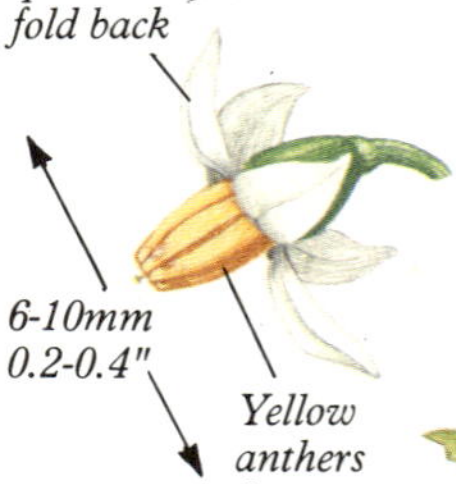

Corolla lobes first spread out, later fold back

6-10mm
0.2-0.4"

Yellow anthers form a cone

Plant is hairless or downy

Flowers are in loose clusters

Do not confuse with *Green Nightshade* which has green ripe berries with large calyces and no black on the stem.

Berries ripen to black: **poisonous**

Oval, shiny leaves are often toothed or lobed

Stem is sometimes blackish

Black Nightshade

Salanum nigrum
Also called: Garden Nightshade, Felonwort.
Habitat: Waste ground, cultivated land, gardens.
Flowers: July to October. Annual.
Distribution: Common throughout England; very local in Ireland and Wales; rare in Scotland.

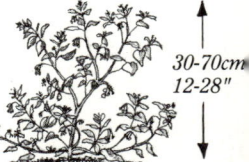

30-70cm
12-28"

A typical, untidy weed

WHITE **5 PETALS**

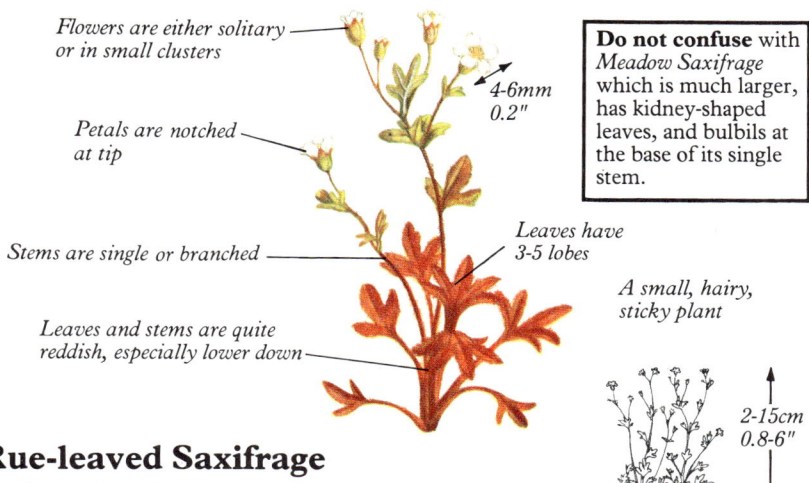

Do not confuse with *Meadow Saxifrage* which is much larger, has kidney-shaped leaves, and bulbils at the base of its single stem.

Flowers are either solitary or in small clusters

Petals are notched at tip

4-6mm 0.2"

Stems are single or branched

Leaves have 3-5 lobes

A small, hairy, sticky plant

Leaves and stems are quite reddish, especially lower down

2-15cm 0.8-6"

Rue-leaved Saxifrage

Saxifraga tridactylites
Habitat: Walls, rocks; dry sandy places.
Flowers: April to June. Annual.
Distribution: Throughout the British Isles; rarer in Scotland.

Size varies from very small to fairly large

Prominent stamens and ovary

Purplish-red anthers

10-15mm 0.4-0.6"

Flower stalks are long and slender

Flowering stems are leafless, slightly hairy and reddish

Small, narrow bracts

Leaves are shiny, fleshy, stalkless and toothed

Narrow petals have 2 yellow spots at base

Sepals turn down

Leaves grow in basal rosettes

Starry Saxifrage

Saxifraga stellaris
Habitat: Wet mountain rocks.
Flowers: June to August. Perennial.
Distribution: Found in mountainous regions throughout the British Isles, especially in the Scottish Highlands.

4-25cm 2-10"

Occurs in small groups

WHITE 5 PETALS

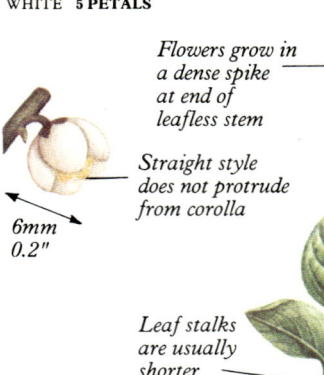

Flowers grow in a dense spike at end of leafless stem

Petals are occasionally pinkish

Straight style does not protrude from corolla

Leafless flower stem

6mm
0.2"

Do not confuse with *Intermediate Wintergreen* which has a protruding style, or with *Larger Wintergreen* which has a curved style.

Oval leaves have shallow, blunt teeth around the edge

Leaf stalks are usually shorter than blades

Common Wintergreen

Pyrola minor
Habitat: Woods, moors, dunes, rock ledges.
Flowers: June to August. Perennial.
Distribution: Local throughout the British Isles, but becoming more local towards the south.

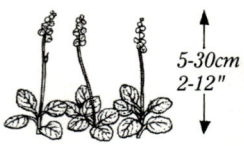

5-30cm
2-12"

Leaves form a basal rosette

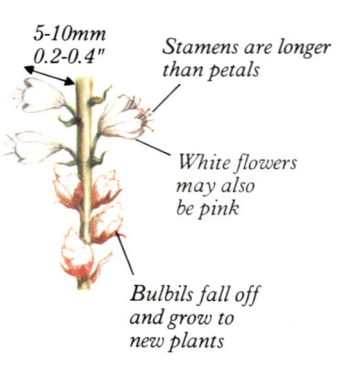

5-10mm
0.2-0.4"

Stamens are longer than petals

White flowers may also be pink

Bulbils fall off and grow to new plants

Top of flower spike has flowers with 5 petals

Bottom of flower spike has bulbils

Slender, upright, weedy-looking plant

Leaf edges often roll under

6-30cm
2.4-12"

Alpine Bistort

Polygonum viviparum
Also called: Viviparous Bistort.
Habitat: On damp rocks, upland grassland.
Flowers: June to August. Perennial.
Distribution: Found on mountains in northern regions.

Several single-stem plants usually occur together

WHITE 5 OR 6 PETALS

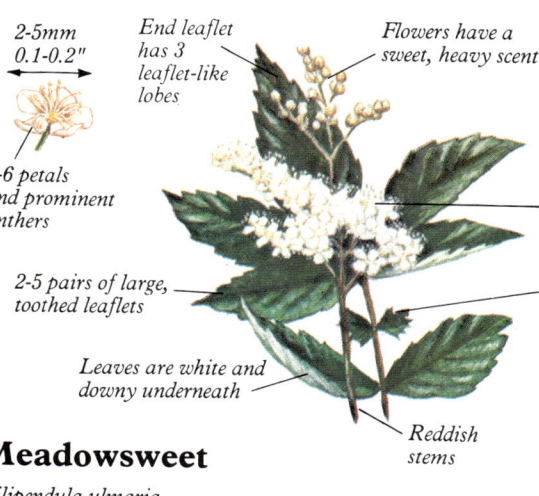

2-5mm
0.1-0.2"

5-6 petals and prominent anthers

2-5 pairs of large, toothed leaflets

Leaves are white and downy underneath

End leaflet has 3 leaflet-like lobes

Flowers have a sweet, heavy scent

Flowers grow in frothy, irregular, many-branched clusters

Small leaflets between large ones

Reddish stems

Do not confuse with *Dropwort* which has larger flowers, more leaflets per stem and prefers a dry environment.

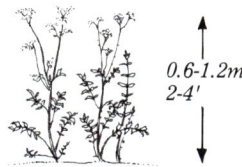

0.6-1.2m
2-4'

Often forms large colonies

Meadowsweet

Filipendula ulmaria
Habitat: Marshes, wet woods and fields, by water.
Flowers: June to September. Perennial.
Distribution: Common throughout the British Isles.

Flowers open in sunlight but are often closed and bud-like

Each flower has a short stalk

Reddish, leafless flower stalks

Flowers have 5 or 6 petals

Sticky red hairs

Round leaves

Long leaf stalk

Insects trapped on sticky hairs are digested by leaf

Do not confuse with other *Sundews* which have leaves much longer than they are broad.

5-25cm
2-10"

Leaves in a basal rosette

Common Sundew

Drosera rotundifolia
Habitat: Bogs, wet and damp heat and moorland.
Flowers: June to August. Perennial.
Distribution: Locally common throughout the British Isles.

WHITE 6+ PETALS

Pale blue and lilac flowers occasionally appear

50-70 stamens in a spiral

Do not confuse with *Wood Sorrel* (p67), or the very rare *Yellow Wood Anemone*.

Solitary flowers have 5-9 petal-like sepals

Each leaf is stalked with 3 lobes

20-40mm
0.8-1.6"

Pink streaks on backs of sepals

Only 3 leaves, about one third the way down stem

Stem is more or less hairless

2 basal leaves appear after flowering

6-30cm
2.4-12"

Wood Anemone

Anemone nemorosa
Also called: Nemony, Wind Flower, Granny's Nightcap.
Habitat: Woodland.
Flowers: March to May. Perennial.
Distribution: Abundant throughout the British Isles except in the far north of Scotland.

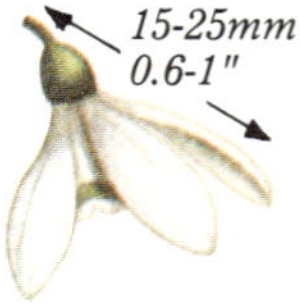

Often forms carpets in woodlands

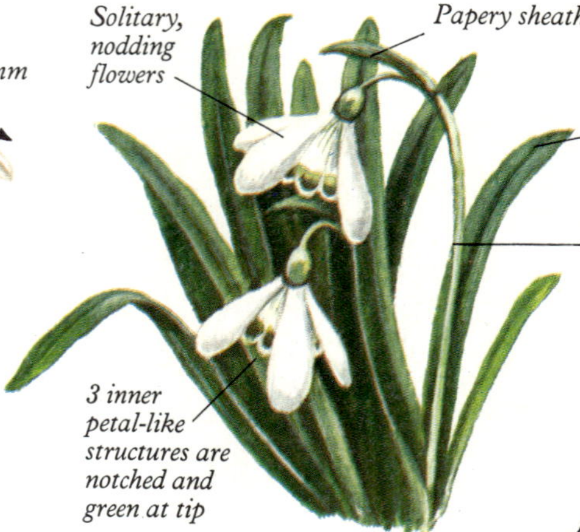

Solitary, nodding flowers

Papery sheath

15-25mm
0.6-1"

2 grooved, angled leaves per flower stem

Leafless flower stem

3 outer petal-like structures are pure white

3 inner petal-like structures are notched and green at tip

Usually the earliest flower of the year

Snowdrop

Galanthus nivalis
Habitat: Damp woods and meadows, often by streams.
Flowers: January to March. Perennial.
Distribution: Local throughout the British Isles.

10-25cm
4-10"

Forms large clumps

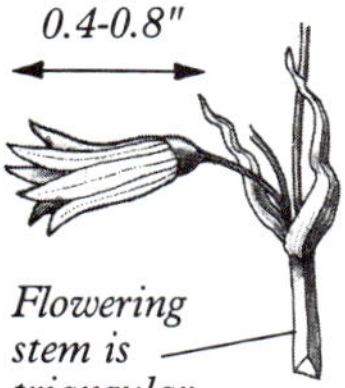

WHITE 6+ PETALS

10-20mm
0.4-0.8"

Flowering stem is triangular

Plant smells strongly of garlic

2-5 leaves each with a central ridge

Flowers hang to one side

Leafless flower stalk

Flowers have 6 petal-like segments each with a central green line

Papery, bract-like structure

No bulbils

Three-cornered Leek
Allium triquetrum
Also called: Triangular-stalked Garlic, Snow Bell.
Habitat: Hedgerows, fields, waste ground.
Flowers: April to June. Perennial.
Distribution: Mainly in south-west England but scattered throughout the British Isles.

20-50cm
8-20"

Often forms large clumps

Usually two pointed shiny leaves

Central ridge

Wide, open flower

No bulbils

2- or 3-angled stem

6 – 20 star-like flowers in a flattish cluster

6 pointed, narrow segments

Papery bract soon falls off

Long leaf stalk

15-20mm
0.6-0.8"

Ramsons
Allium ursinum
Also called: Bear's Garlic, Wild Garlic, Ramps.
Habitat: Damp woodlands, shady places.
Flowers: April to June. Perennial.
Distribution: Locally common throughout the British Isles except in the far north and Channel Islands.

10-45cm
4-18"

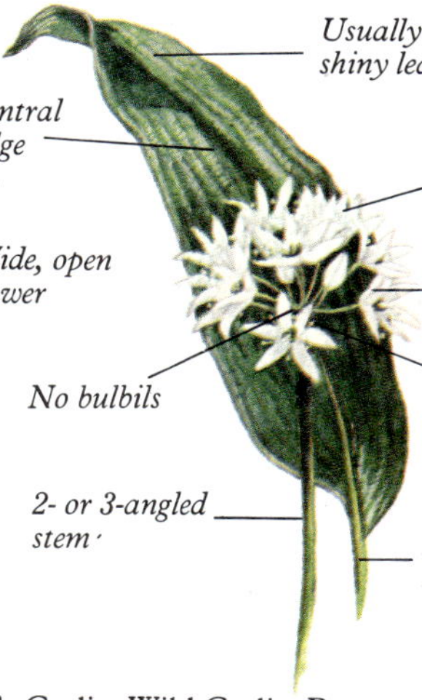

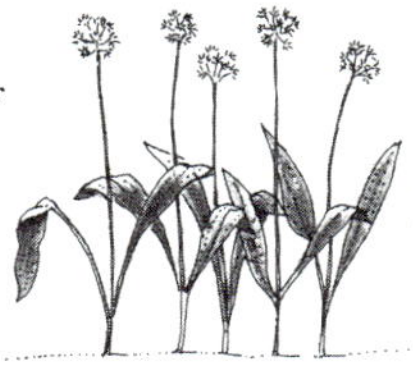

Often forms dense carpets with a strong smell of garlic

WHITE **COMPOSITE**

Daisy

Bellis perennis
Habitat: Short grassland, especially garden lawns.
Flowers: February to November. Perennial.
Distribution: Common throughout the British Isles.

Large numbers usually grow together

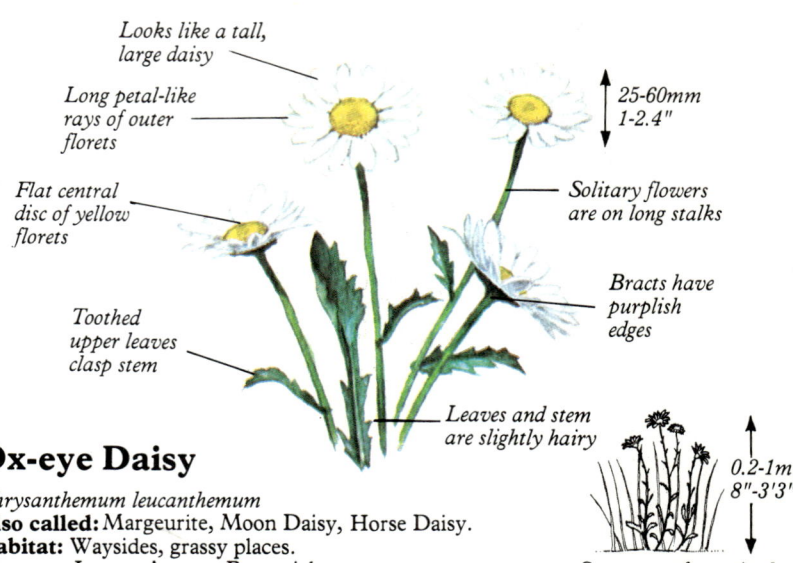

Ox-eye Daisy

Chrysanthemum leucanthemum
Also called: Margeurite, Moon Daisy, Horse Daisy.
Habitat: Waysides, grassy places.
Flowers: June to August. Perennial.
Distribution: Common throughout the British Isles.

Stems are often mixed with long grass

WHITE COMPOSITE

10-25cm
0.4-1"

Loose clusters of flowerheads on long stalks

Flat central disc of yellow florets

Plant is strongly scented and downy

Petal-like rays of outer florets are broad

Leaves have deep, toothed lobes and are often downy

Ribbed stems are branched at top

25-80cm
10-32"

Feverfew
Tanacetum parthenium
Habitat: Waste ground, hedgebanks, walls, grassland.
Flowers: July to August. Perennial.
Distribution: Common throughout the British Isles.

Looks like a leafy, tall, well-branched daisy

Do not confuse with other *Chamomiles* and *Mayweeds* that differ in hairiness, scent, angle of rays, and bract colours. *Rayless Mayweed (Pineapple Weed)* has only the central cone of yellow florets with no white rays.

RAYLESS MAYWEED

10-25mm
0.4-1"

Central disc of yellow florets is domed

Bracts have light green edge

Petal-like rays of outer florets bend back

Stem is hairless, well branched

Feathery, very finely divided leaves

Whole plant has a pleasant smell

15-60cm
6-24"

Scented Mayweed
Matricaria recutita
Also called: Wild Chamomile, Maithen.
Habitat: Fields, waste places.
Flowers: June to July. Annual.
Distribution: Local throughout the British Isles.

A bushy, untidy plant with many branched stems

WHITE COMPOSITE/LIPPED

4-6mm / 0.2"

6 ray florets

Each 'flower' is a flowerhead with disc and ray florets

Flowers grow in flat-topped clusters

Long, narrow, feathery leaves

Basal leaves are stalked

Stem is furrowed, woody and hairy

Plant has fairly strong scent

8-60cm / 3-24"

Yarrow

Achillea millefolium
Also called: Milfoil, Angel Flower, Bunch o' Daisies.
Habitat: Grassy areas, waysides, disturbed ground.
Flowers: June to October. Perennial.
Distribution: Common throughout the British Isles.

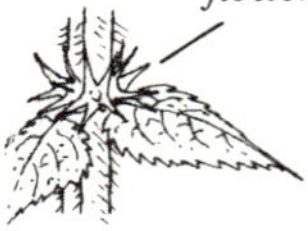

Often forms large patches

Whorls of calyces remain after flowers drop

Resembles a nettle without the sting

Do not confuse with *Spotted Dead-nettle* which has pinkish-purple flowers, and leaves with a large, whitish blotch.

Conspicuous white flowers are in whorls up the stem

Black markings around stem and calyces under flower whorls

Top lip is hooded and hairy

Leaves are slightly hairy, and always stalked

Leaves grow in opposite pairs

Stem is 4-sided and hairy

White Dead-nettle

Lamium album
Habitat: Hedges, waste ground.
Flowers: May to September. Perennial.
Distribution: Common in England; local in Wales, southern Scotland and eastern Ireland.

20-60cm / 8-24"

Often found in large clumps

WHITE **LIPPED/TUBULAR OR BELL**

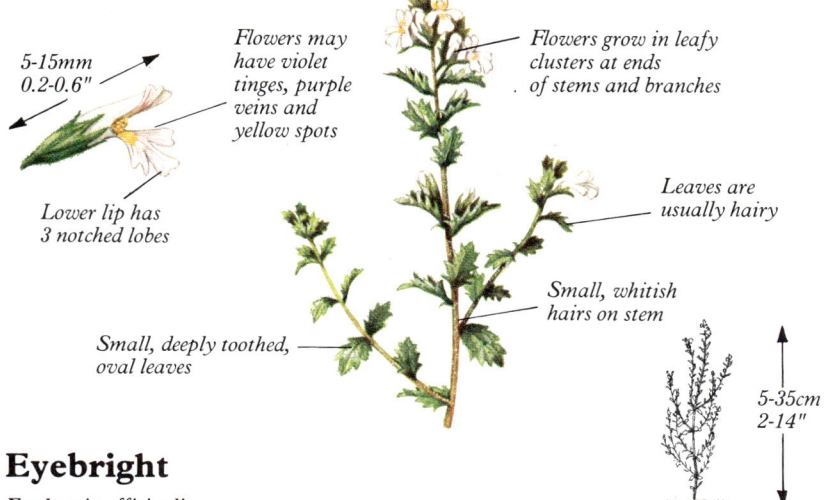

Eyebright

Euphrasia officinalis
Habitat: Grassy, open places.
Flowers: June to October. Annual.
Distribution: Common throughout the British Isles.

Do not confuse with *Angular Solomon's Seal* which has angled stems and scented flowers, or *Whorled Solomon's Seal* which has leaves in whorls.

Common Solomon's Seal

Polygonatum multiflorum
Habitat: Woods, gardens.
Flowers: April to June. Perennial.
Distribution: Scattered throughout the British Isles but common in central southern England.

WHITE   **TUBULAR OR BELL**

6-8mm
0.3"

Bell-shaped flowers fall to one side of stem

Leaves are broad, long and pointed, with parallel veins; usually 2 per stem

Flower stem grows out from alongside the leaf stems

Each flower has a short, dry bract

*The round, red berries are **poisonous***

Lily-of-the-Valley

Convallaria majalis
Habitat: Dry woods, gardens.
Flowers: May to June. Perennial.
Distribution: Local in England and south-east Wales; very local in Scotland and Ireland.

8-20cm
3-8"

Often forms large patches

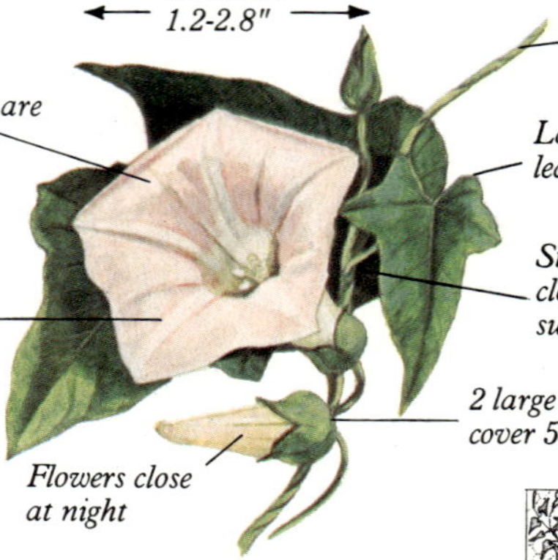

30-70mm
1.2-2.8"

Stems can be hairless or slightly downy

Large flowers are borne singly

Large, arrow-shaped leaves

Funnel-shaped corolla can be white or pinkish

Stems twine anti-clockwise around supports

2 large bracts cover 5 sepals

Flowers close at night

Greater Bindweed

Calystegia sepium
Also called: Bellbine, Hedge Bindweed, Convulvulus.
Habitat: Walls, hedgerows, waste places, gardens.
Flowers: June to September. Perennial.
Distribution: Common throughout the British Isles.

1-3m
3'3"-9'9"

A vigorous plant; spreads for long distances

WHITE PEA/UMBELLIFER

White Clover

Trifolium repens
Also called: Wild White, Dutch Clover, Kentish Clover.
Habitat: Grassy places.
Flowers: May to September. Perennial.
Distribution: Common throughout the British Isles.

Forms large patches; stems often hidden in grass

Great Masterwort

Astrantia major
Also called: Melancholy Gentleman, Mountain Sanicle.
Habitat: Meadows. Wood edges.
Flowers: June to September. Perennial.
Distribution: Rare throughout the British Isles

Grows in patches

WHITE **UMBELLIFER**

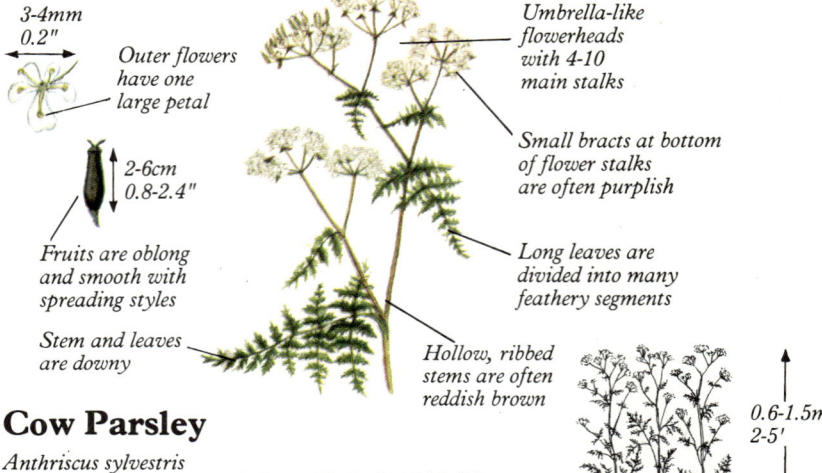

3-4mm
0.2"

Outer flowers have one large petal

Umbrella-like flowerheads with 4-10 main stalks

2-6cm
0.8-2.4"

Small bracts at bottom of flower stalks are often purplish

Fruits are oblong and smooth with spreading styles

Long leaves are divided into many feathery segments

Stem and leaves are downy

Hollow, ribbed stems are often reddish brown

0.6-1.5m
2-5'

Cow Parsley

Anthriscus sylvestris
Also called: Keck, Lady's Lace, Kelk, Rabbit's Meat.
Habitat: Hedgerows, wood edges, roadsides, ditches.
Flowers: April to June. Biennial.
Distribution: Common throughout the British Isles.

Often covers large patches giving a frothy appearance

2-3mm
0.1"

Outer petals are longer than inner ones

Flowerheads have 5-12 long main stalks

Bracts at base of main stalks and flower stalks

Purplish fruit is covered with hooked spines

1.5-4cm
0.6-1.6"

Solid stems have coarse, bent-back hairs

Leaves are not as feathery as Cow Parsley

Stem is marked with lines

Upright Hedge Parsley

Torilis japonica
Habitat: Hedgebanks, grassy places.
Flowers: July to August. Annual.
Distribution: Common throughout the British Isles.

0.5-1.25m
1'8"-4'2"

Bushy appearance; flowers later than Cow Parsley

WHITE   UMBELLIFER

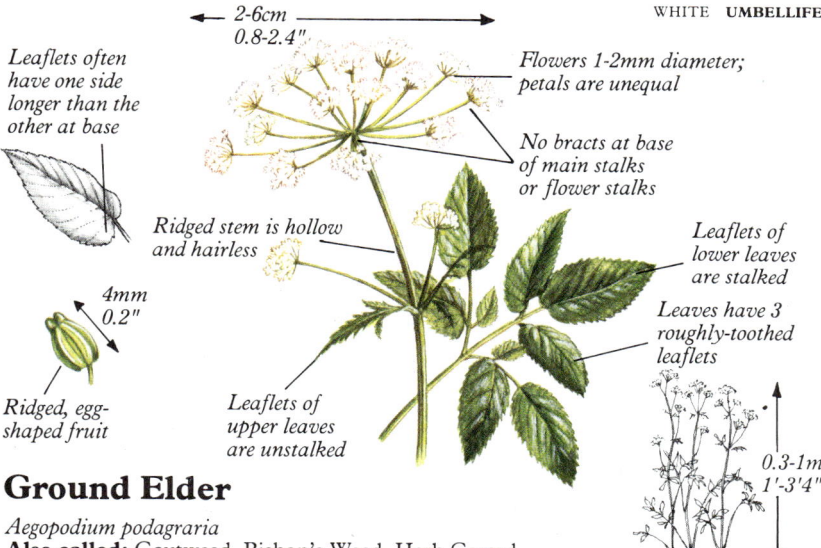

Leaflets often have one side longer than the other at base

← 2-6cm →
0.8-2.4"

Flowers 1-2mm diameter; petals are unequal

No bracts at base of main stalks or flower stalks

Ridged stem is hollow and hairless

4mm
0.2"

Leaflets of lower leaves are stalked

Ridged, egg-shaped fruit

Leaves have 3 roughly-toothed leaflets

Leaflets of upper leaves are unstalked

0.3-1m
1'-3'4"

Ground Elder

Aegopodium podagraria
Also called: Goutweed, Bishop's Weed, Herb Gerard.
Flowers: May to August. Perennial.
Distribution: Common throughout the British Isles.

Often forms large patches

Large leaves have broad, hairy, wavy, lobed leaflets

Small bracts grow at base of flower stems only

Do not confuse with *Giant Hogweed* which is up to 5m/16' high with red-spotted stems to 10cm/4" diameter.

5-10mm
0.2-0.4"

Petals are deeply notched; those of outer flowers are unequal

Flowerheads have 7-20 main stalks

Leaf stalks have a broad, veined sheath at base

Rounded fruit

Hogweed

Heracleum sphondylium
Also called: Cow Parsnip, Keck, Kesh, Rabbit's Meat.
Habitat: Grassy places, roadsides, open woodland.
Flowers: June to September. Biennial.
Distribution: Common throughout the British Isles.

0.5-2m
1'8"-6'6"

Often bushy with long branches

WHITE **UMBELLIFER**

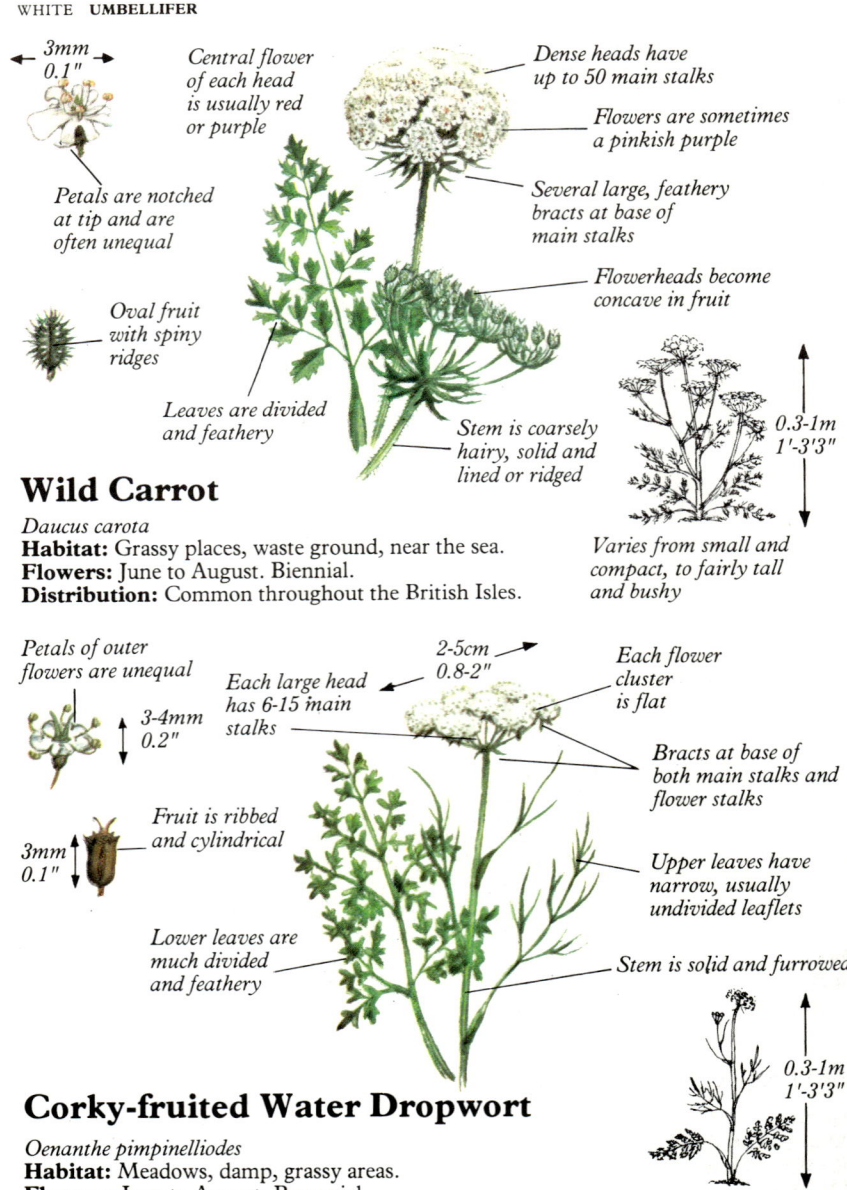

3mm / 0.1"

Central flower of each head is usually red or purple

Dense heads have up to 50 main stalks

Flowers are sometimes a pinkish purple

Petals are notched at tip and are often unequal

Several large, feathery bracts at base of main stalks

Oval fruit with spiny ridges

Flowerheads become concave in fruit

Leaves are divided and feathery

Stem is coarsely hairy, solid and lined or ridged

0.3-1m / 1'-3'3"

Wild Carrot

Daucus carota
Habitat: Grassy places, waste ground, near the sea.
Flowers: June to August. Biennial.
Distribution: Common throughout the British Isles.

Varies from small and compact, to fairly tall and bushy

Petals of outer flowers are unequal

3-4mm / 0.2"

Each large head has 6-15 main stalks

2-5cm / 0.8-2"

Each flower cluster is flat

Bracts at base of both main stalks and flower stalks

Fruit is ribbed and cylindrical

3mm / 0.1"

Upper leaves have narrow, usually undivided leaflets

Lower leaves are much divided and feathery

Stem is solid and furrowed

0.3-1m / 1'-3'3"

Corky-fruited Water Dropwort

Oenanthe pimpinelloides
Habitat: Meadows, damp, grassy areas.
Flowers: June to August. Perennial.
Distribution: Local in southern England and County Cork.

Upright, branched plant

GREEN 0-3 PETALS

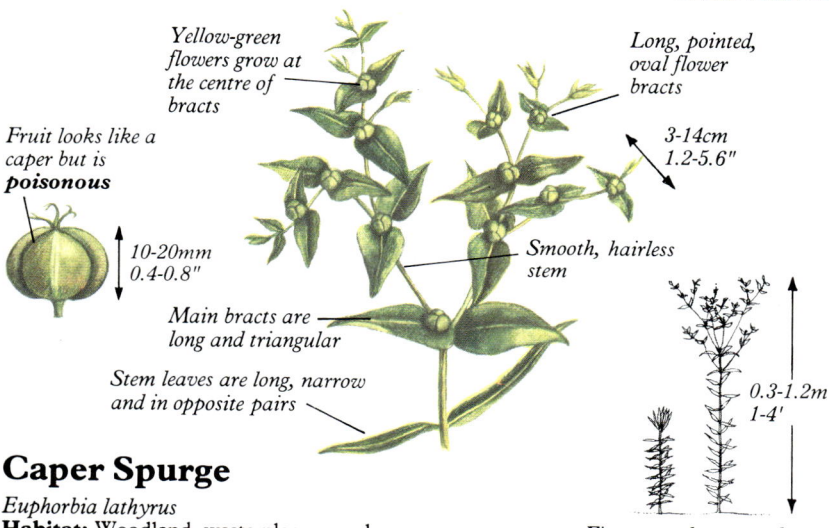

Yellow-green flowers grow at the centre of bracts

Long, pointed, oval flower bracts

*Fruit looks like a caper but is **poisonous***

3-14cm 1.2-5.6"

10-20mm 0.4-0.8"

Smooth, hairless stem

Main bracts are long and triangular

Stem leaves are long, narrow and in opposite pairs

0.3-1.2m 1-4'

Caper Spurge
Euphorbia lathyrus
Habitat: Woodland, waste places, gardens.
Flowers: June to July. Usually biennial.
Distribution: Scattered throughout the British Isles.

First year plants are short and leafy; flowering plants are very tall

Yellow-green bracts turn reddish

Whorl of bracts below flower cluster

6-15mm 0.2-0.6"

Flower

Leafy secondary stems

Stem and leaves are hairless

Flower bracts are not joined

Narrow, alternate leaves

Cypress Spurge
Euphorbia cyparissias
Habitat: Grass and scrubland, gardens.
Flowers: May to August. Perennial.
Distribution: Scattered throughout England and Wales; rare in Scotland and Ireland.

15-30cm 6-12"

Plant forms large patches

GREEN 0-3 PETALS

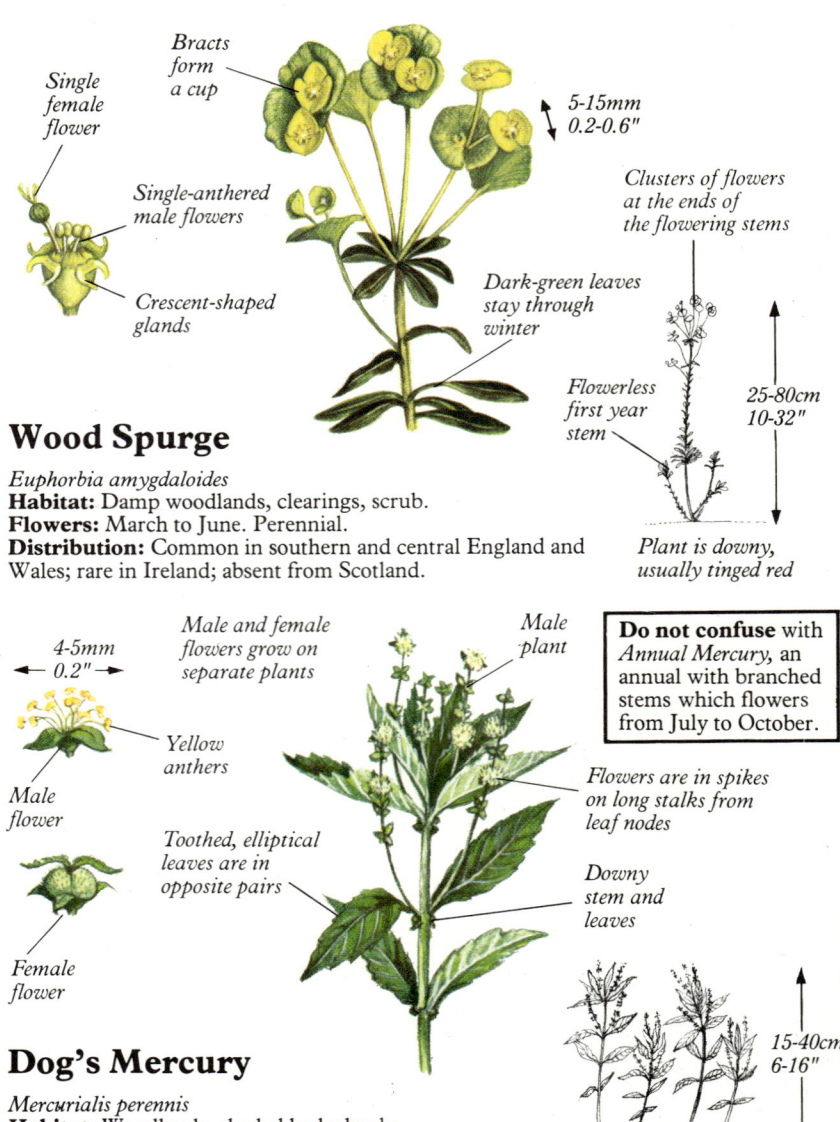

Wood Spurge

Euphorbia amygdaloides
Habitat: Damp woodlands, clearings, scrub.
Flowers: March to June. Perennial.
Distribution: Common in southern and central England and Wales; rare in Ireland; absent from Scotland.

Do not confuse with *Annual Mercury*, an annual with branched stems which flowers from July to October.

Dog's Mercury

Mercurialis perennis
Habitat: Woodlands, shaded hedgebanks.
Flowers: February to April. Perennial.
Distribution: Common throughout the British Isles except in far northern Scotland and Ireland.

GREEN **0-3 PETALS**

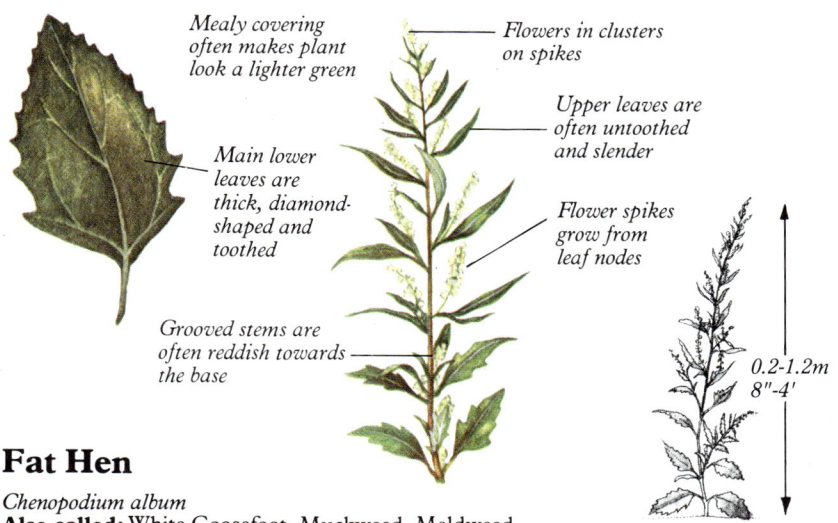

1-2mm
0.1"

Male and female flowers are on different plants

4 stamens

Male flower

Female flower

Plant is covered in painful, stinging hairs

Flowers grow in dangling spikes

Distinctly veined leaves have toothed edges

Pointed, oval leaves are in opposite pairs

4-angled stem

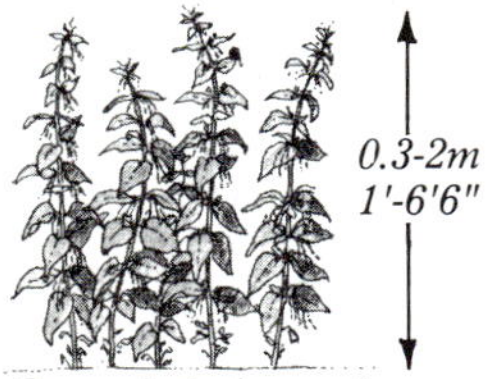

0.3-2m
1'-6'6"

Grows in large patches

Nettle

Urtica dioica
Habitat: Hedges, woods, waste ground, grassy places.
Flowers: June to September. Perennial.
Distribution: Common throughout the British Isles.

Mealy covering often makes plant look a lighter green

Flowers in clusters on spikes

Upper leaves are often untoothed and slender

Main lower leaves are thick, diamond-shaped and toothed

Flower spikes grow from leaf nodes

Grooved stems are often reddish towards the base

0.2-1.2m
8"-4'

Fat Hen

Chenopodium album
Also called: White Goosefoot, Muckweed, Meldweed.
Habitat: Waste places, waysides, cultivated ground.
Flowers: July to October. Annual.
Distribution: Common throughout the British Isles.

A weedier, less stately plant than Good King Henry (p86)

GREEN 0-3 PETALS

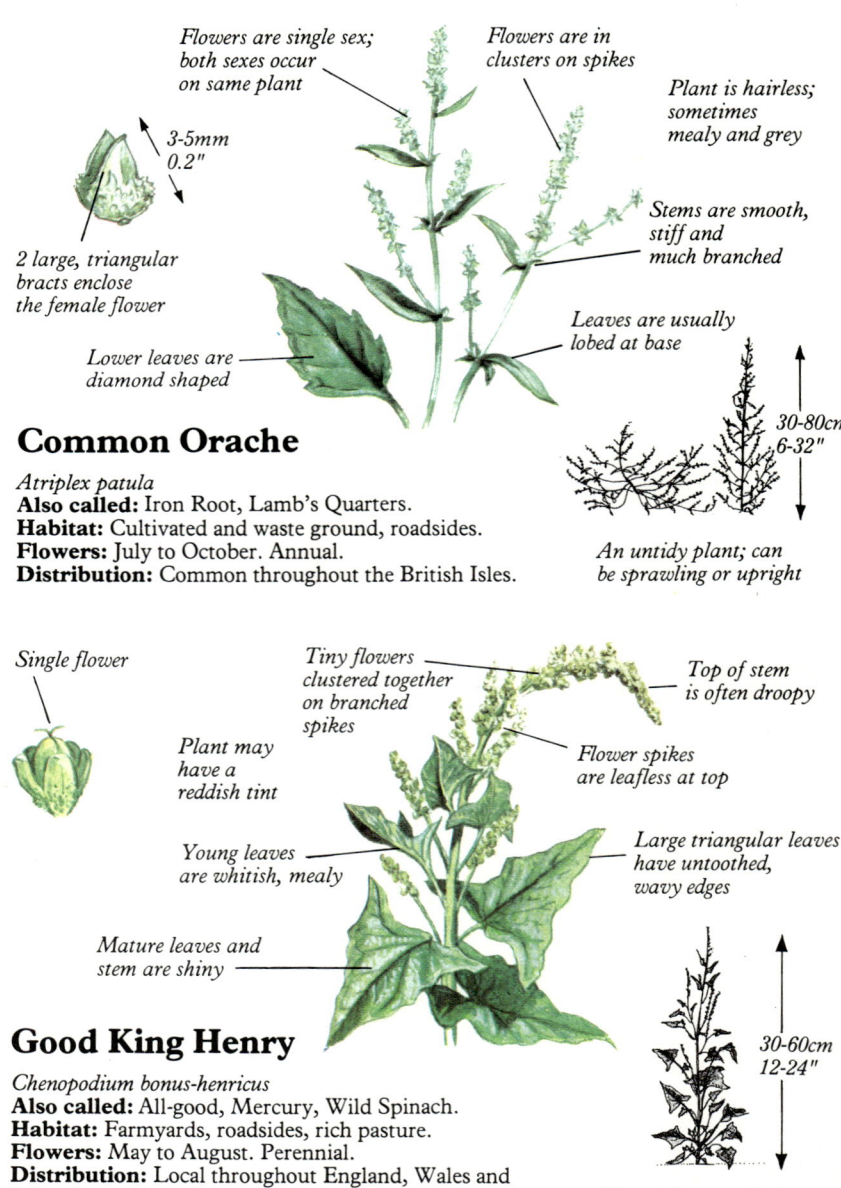

Flowers are single sex; both sexes occur on same plant

Flowers are in clusters on spikes

Plant is hairless; sometimes mealy and grey

3-5mm 0.2"

2 large, triangular bracts enclose the female flower

Stems are smooth, stiff and much branched

Lower leaves are diamond shaped

Leaves are usually lobed at base

30-80cm 6-32"

Common Orache

Atriplex patula
Also called: Iron Root, Lamb's Quarters.
Habitat: Cultivated and waste ground, roadsides.
Flowers: July to October. Annual.
Distribution: Common throughout the British Isles.

An untidy plant; can be sprawling or upright

Single flower

Tiny flowers clustered together on branched spikes

Top of stem is often droopy

Plant may have a reddish tint

Flower spikes are leafless at top

Young leaves are whitish, mealy

Large triangular leaves have untoothed, wavy edges

Mature leaves and stem are shiny

Good King Henry

Chenopodium bonus-henricus
Also called: All-good, Mercury, Wild Spinach.
Habitat: Farmyards, roadsides, rich pasture.
Flowers: May to August. Perennial.
Distribution: Local throughout England, Wales and Ireland; rare in northern and western Scotland.

30-60cm 12-24"

Plant is large and vigorous

GREEN 0-3 PETALS

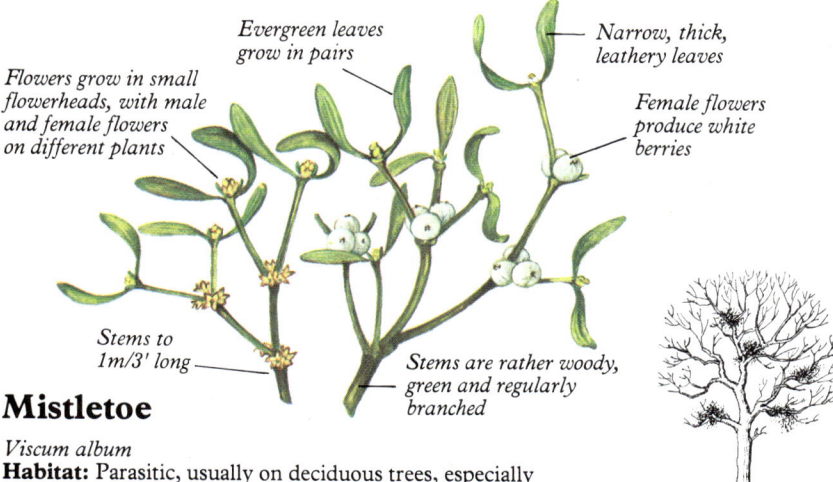

Mistletoe
Viscum album
Habitat: Parasitic, usually on deciduous trees, especially apple and poplar.
Flowers: February to April. Perennial.
Distribution: Common throughout England and Wales, especially in the south; absent from Scotland and Ireland.

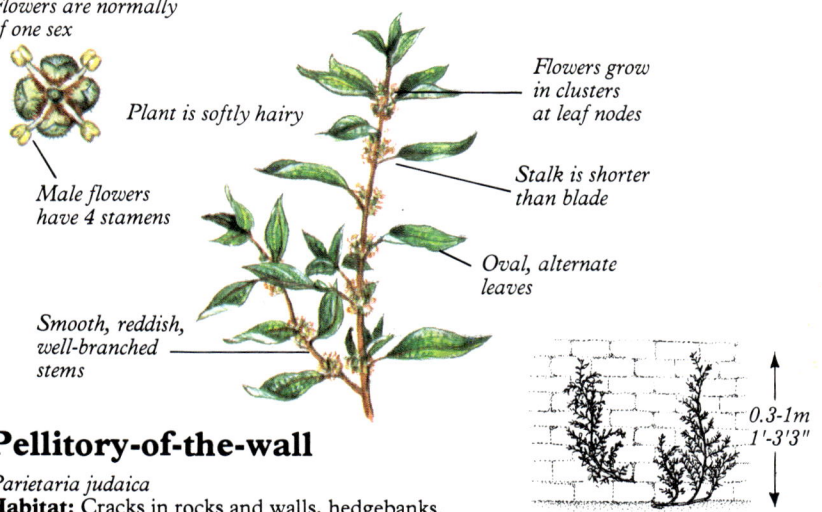

Pellitory-of-the-wall
Parietaria judaica
Habitat: Cracks in rocks and walls, hedgebanks.
Flowers: June to October. Perennial.
Distribution: Local throughout England, Wales, and Ireland and in southern Scotland only.

GREEN 0-3 PETALS

Large pale-green hood

Purple, club-like spike is rarely yellowish

Shiny arrow-shaped leaves usually have black spots

3-5cm
1.2-2.0"

Long-stalked leaves appear before flowers

Flowers are hidden in base of hood

Spike of brilliant red berries is present from July to September: **poisonous**

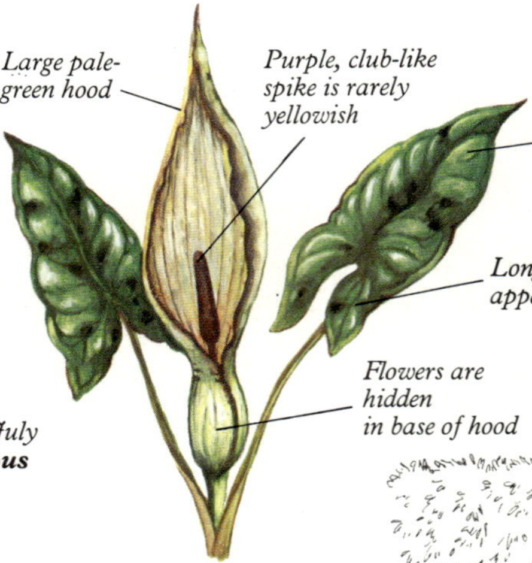

Cuckoo Pint
Arum maculatum
Also called: Lords and Ladies, Wild Arum.
Habitat: Woods, shaded hedgebanks.
Flowers: April to May. Perennial.
Distribution: Common throughout England, Wales and Ireland; absent from northern Scotland.

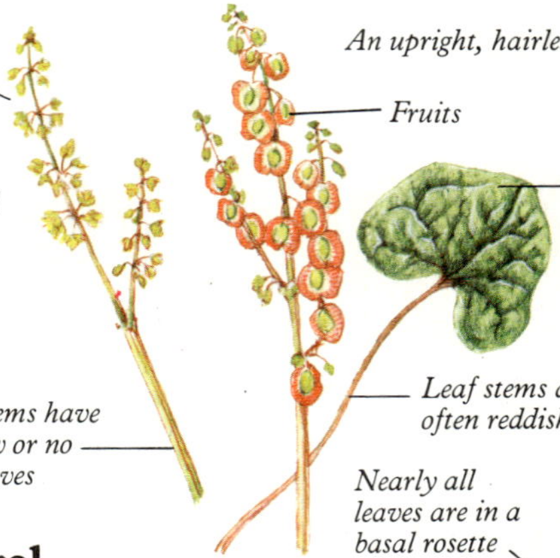

20-50cm
8-20"

Found singly or in groups

Flowers grow in a branched spike

An upright, hairless plant

Fruits

Fruits have broad reddish wings

Kidney-shaped, glossy, fleshy leaves

3-5mm
0.1"-0.2"

Stems have few or no leaves

Leaf stems are often reddish

Nearly all leaves are in a basal rosette

Mountain Sorrel
Oxyria digyna
Habitat: Damp, rocky areas on mountains.
Flowers: July to August. Perennial.
Distribution: Found on mountains over 600m/2000' in north Wales, the Lake District and Scotland.

5-30cm
2-12"

Plant grows in small, tufted clumps

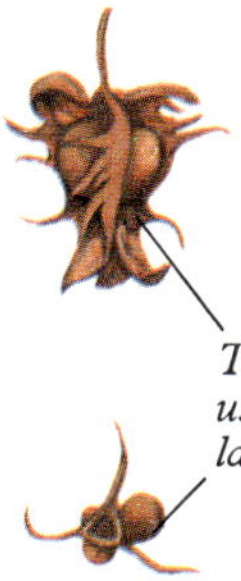

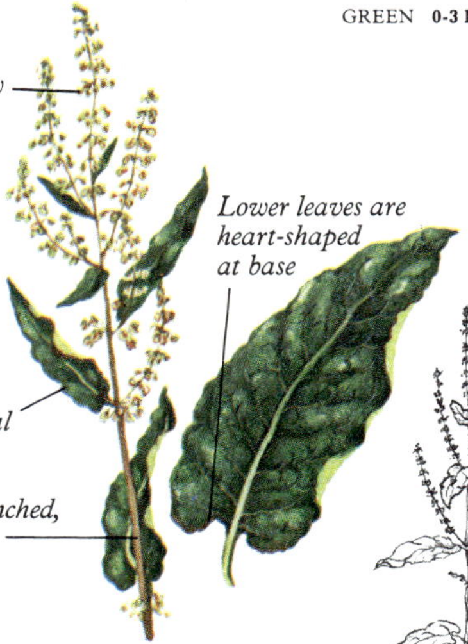

GREEN **0-3 PETALS/4 PETALS**

Broad-leaved Dock

Rumex obtusifolius
Habitat: Waste ground, woods, fields, hedgebanks.
Flowers: June to October. Perennial.
Distribution: Common throughout the British Isles.

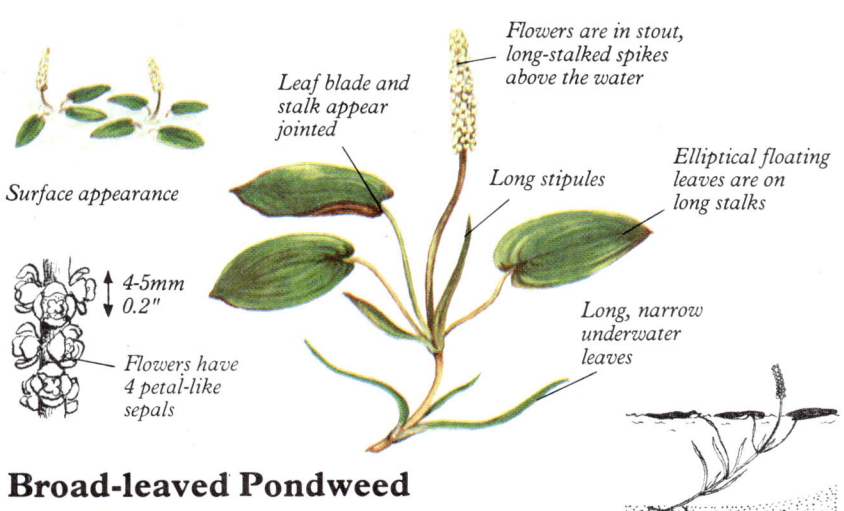

Broad-leaved Pondweed

Potamogeton natans
Habitat: Still and slow-running fresh water.
Flowers: May to September. Perennial.
Distribution: Common throughout the British Isles.

89

GREEN 4 PETALS/5 PETALS

40-70mm
1.6-2.8"

Dark carpels later develop into fruit

Narrow stamens have long anthers

4-6 very narrow petals

4-6 narrow, pointed sepals

Usually 4 leaves are in a whorl at top of stem

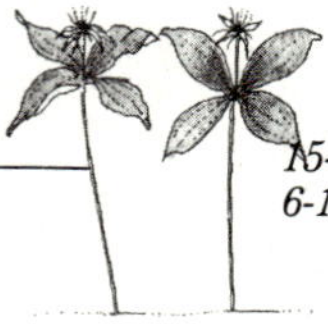

Fruit is a black berry: **poisonous**

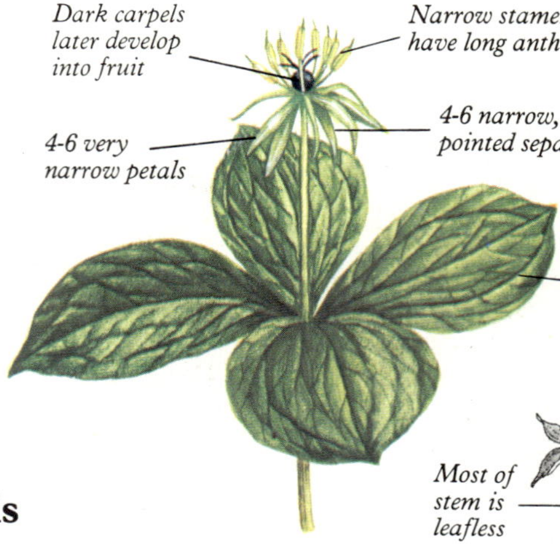

Most of stem is leafless

15-40cm
6-16"

Often grows in large groups

Herb Paris

Paris quadrifolia
Habitat: Damp woods.
Flowers: May to June. Perennial.
Distribution: Scattered throughout the British Isles.

3-5mm
0.2"

Male flower

Fruit is a shiny, pale red berry: **poisonous**

Male flowers are in long, stalked spikes

Male flowers have 6 stamens; female flowers have one style

Large, heart-shaped, shiny leaves

Short, nearly stalkless female flower spikes have fewer flowers

Long, slender, hairless stems twine clockwise

Black Bryony

Tamus communis
Habitat: Wood edges, hedgerows, scrub.
Flowers: May to July. Perennial.
Distribution: Locally common in England and Wales; rare in Ireland and absent from most of Scotland.

Stems grow to 4m/13'

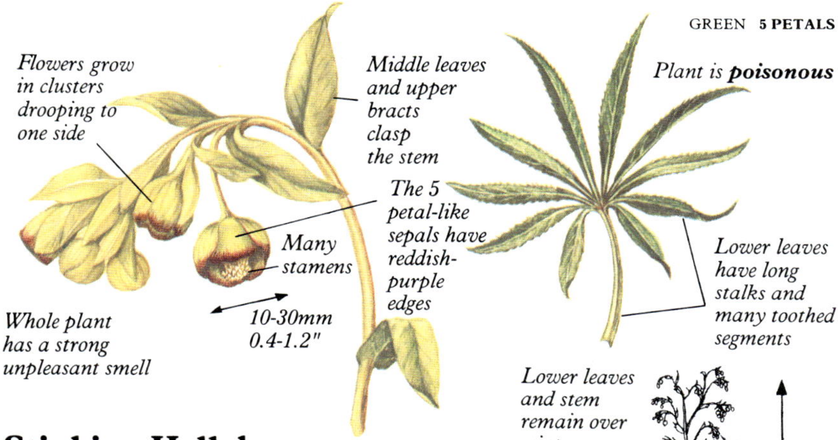

GREEN **5 PETALS**

Flowers grow in clusters drooping to one side

Middle leaves and upper bracts clasp the stem

*Plant is **poisonous***

The 5 petal-like sepals have reddish-purple edges

Many stamens

10-30mm 0.4-1.2"

Lower leaves have long stalks and many toothed segments

Whole plant has a strong unpleasant smell

Lower leaves and stem remain over winter

20-80cm 8-32"

Stinking Hellebore
Helleborus foetidus
Also called: Bear's Foot, Setterwort, Setter-grass.
Habitat: Woodland and scrub on chalky soils.
Flowers: January to March. Perennial.
Distribution: Very local in southern and western England and Wales; found elsewhere as a garden escape.

No basal leaves; may form a large bush after a few years

30-50mm 1.2-2"

Petal-like sepals open out wide

2-4 drooping flowers

Stem leaves have deep, toothed segments

Nectaries

Many stamens with yellow anthers are clearly visible

Usually 2 long-stalked, deeply divided basal leaves at flowering time

Plant does not last over winter. **Poisonous**

Green Hellebore
Helleborus viridis
Also called: Bear's Foot, Fellon-grass, Green Lily.
Habitat: Woods, scrubland, cultivated in gardens.
Flowers: March to April. Perennial.
Distribution: Local, mainly in England and Wales.

10-50cm 4-20"

Grows in patches

GREEN 5 PETALS

*3-5cm
1.2-2"*

Female 'cone' enlarges to form the fruit, or 'Hop'; matures from green to light brown

Male flowers are in branched clusters

*4-6mm
0.2"*

Cone-like groups of bracts contain female flowers

Leaves with 3-5 well-toothed lobes

*15-20mm
0.6-0.8"*

Square stems twine clockwise

Roughly hairy stem and leaves

Hop

Humulus lupulus
Habitat: Hedgebanks. Often cultivated.
Flowers: July to August. Perennial.
Distribution: Wild throughout Britain. Cultivated (mainly in Kent and Worcestershire) for brewing ale.

Twining stems can reach 7m/23' in length

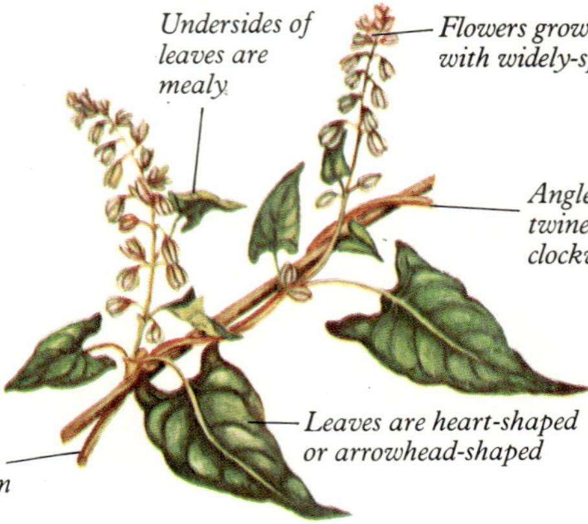

Undersides of leaves are mealy

Flowers grow in long spikes with widely-spaced leaves

*4-6mm
0.2"*

Angled stem twines clockwise

Dull black fruit has narrow, white wings

Stem is often reddish brown

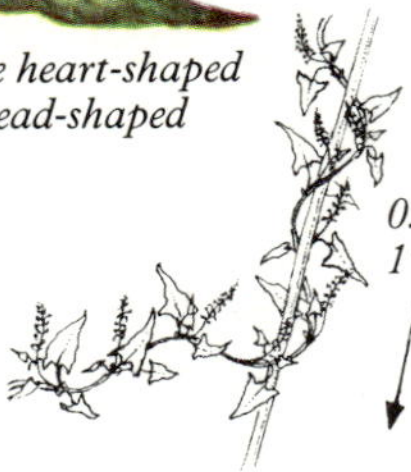

Leaves are heart-shaped or arrowhead-shaped

*0.3-1m
1'-3'3"*

Black Bindweed

Bilderdykia convolvulus
Also called: Climbing Buckwheat, Cornbind, Lap-love.
Habitat: Waste and cultivated ground, gardens.
Flowers: July to October. Annual.
Distribution: Common throughout the British Isles.

Scrambles over ground or climbs supports

Ribwort Plantain

Plantago lanceolata
Also called: Cocks and Hens, Ribgrass, Soldiers.
Habitat: Roadsides, grassy and waste places, lawns.
Flowers: April to September. Perennial.
Distribution: Common throughout the British Isles.

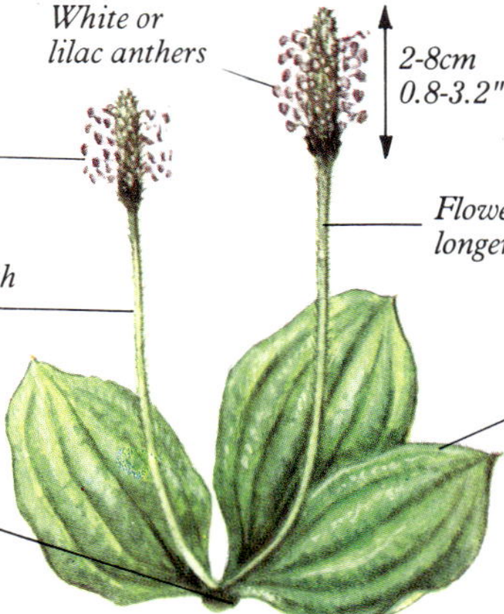

Hoary Plantain

Plantago media
Habitat: Grassy places, lawns.
Flowers: May to August. Perennial.
Distribution: Fairly common in central and southern England; rarer northwards and in Ireland.

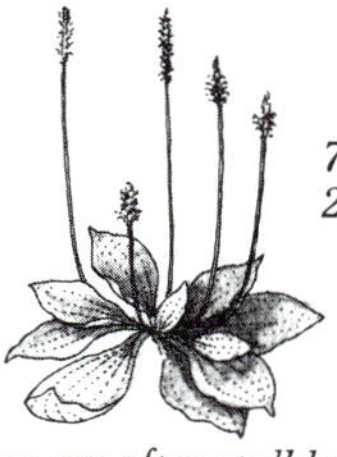

GREEN COMPOSITE/LIPPED

Long, protruding stamens have coloured anthers

Long, dense flower spike is as long as or longer than stem

Anthers are first lilac, later yellow

5-20cm
2-8"

Broad, oval leaves are distinctly ribbed

Leaves narrow abruptly to a stalk as long as blade

2-4mm
0.1"

Tiny flowers are typical of plantains

Plant is hairless or downy

Flowering stems are only just longer than leaves

Greater Plantain

Plantago major
Also called: Ratstail, Way-bread, Hardheads.
Habitat: Open and cultivated ground, lawns.
Flowers: May to September. Perennial.
Distribution: Common throughout the British Isles.

10-50cm
4-20"

Leaves usually lie close to the ground

Red-brown stamens are very prominent

Flowers usually hang to one side

No top lip

Flowers are in pairs on long, stalked spikes

Bottom lip has 5 lobes

7-9mm
0.3"

Stem is square and branched

Stem and leaves are downy and hairy

Leaves are oval, stalked, and heart-shaped at base

Leaves are toothed and wrinkled

Wood Sage

Teucrium scorodonia
Also called: Wood Germander, Wild Sage.
Habitat: Woods, scrub, grassland, dunes.
Flowers: July to September. Perennial.
Distribution: Common throughout the British Isles.

15-60cm
6-24"

Plant has many stems

GREEN **LIPPED**

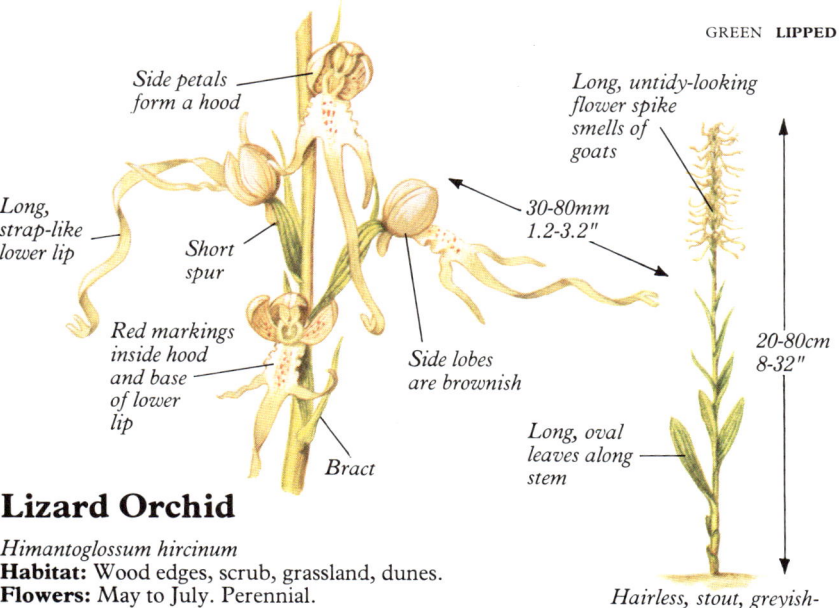

Lizard Orchid

Himantoglossum hircinum
Habitat: Wood edges, scrub, grassland, dunes.
Flowers: May to July. Perennial.
Distribution: Very rare; found only in southern England.

Common Twayblade

Listera ovata
Habitat: Damp woods, shady grassland, dunes.
Flowers: June to July. Perennial.
Distribution: Locally common throughout the British Isles.

YELLOW 0-3 PETALS/4 PETALS

2-4mm
0.1-0.2"

Very long upright stamens give a frothy look

Flowers grow in dense, upright clusters

Leaflets are toothed at ends

4 small sepals often fall off as flower opens

Leaves have many stalked, wedge-shaped leaflets

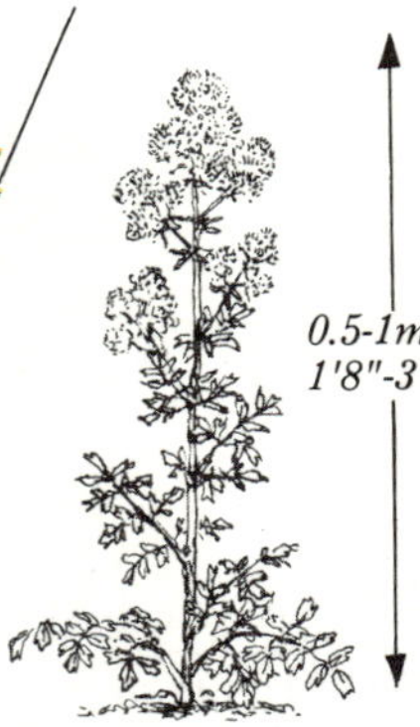

Common Meadow Rue

Thalictrum flavum
Habitat: Damp meadows, fens, by water.
Flowers: June to August. Perennial.
Distribution: Local throughout the British Isles.

0.5-1m
1'8"-3'3"

Tall, upright, robust plant; often looks bushy

Often an orange blotch at base of petals

2-3 flowers grow together; pale to deep yellow

80-100mm
0.3-0.4"

Fruits are bright green capsules

3 large petal-like structures often have purple-brown markings

Sword-shaped leaves have central rib

Sheathing bracts

Yellow Flag

Iris pseudacorus
Habitat: Shallow water; marshy, swampy, wet ground.
Flowers: May to July. Perennial.
Distribution: Common throughout the British Isles.

0.4-1.5m
1'4"-5'

Grows in large patches, usually in shallow water

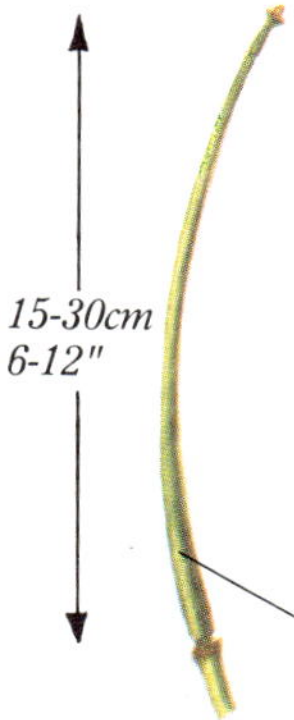

YELLOW **4 PETALS**

60-90mm
2.4-3.6"

Large yellow flowers are solitary on short stalks

Rounded petals

15-30cm
6-12"

Pod and plant are grey-green

Leaves are hairy, wavy and lobed

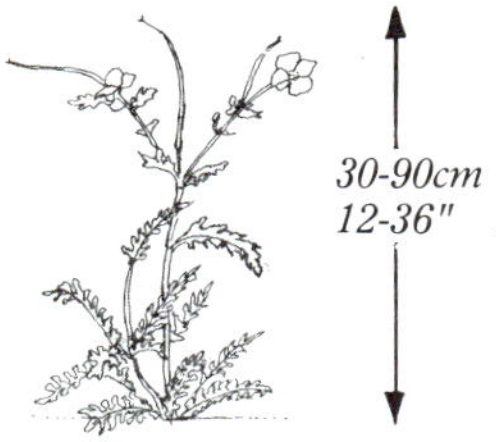

Fruit pod is very long and curved

Yellow Horned Poppy

Glaucium flavum
Habitat: Shingly beaches, coastal waste areas.
Flowers: June to September. Biennial or perennial.
Distribution: Found around the coasts of the British Isles except in northern Scotland.

30-90cm
12-36"

Stem is upright and branched

Buds have red-striped sepals

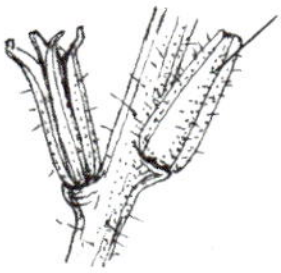

80-100mm
3.2-4"

Many buds

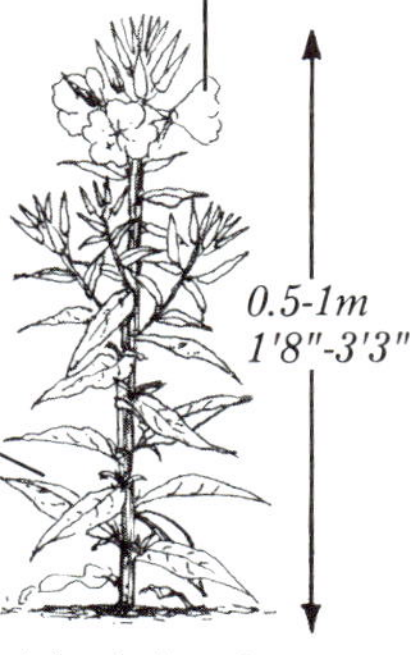

Flowers open in late afternoon

Fruit capsules are hairy

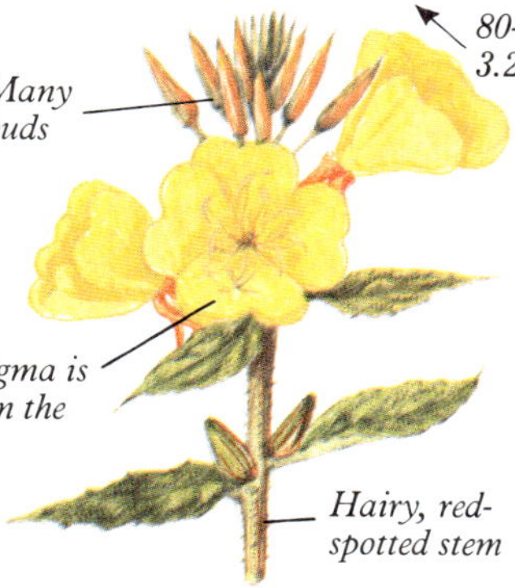

4-lobed stigma is longer than the 8 anthers

Hairy, red-spotted stem

Large-flowered Evening Primrose

Oenothera erythrosepala
Habitat: Roadsides, banks, waste ground, gardens.
Flowers: June to September. Usually biennial.
Distribution: Mainly in southern England and Wales; scattered as an escape from cultivation elsewhere.

Narrow leaves

0.5-1m
1'8"-3'3"

Upright, hairy plant

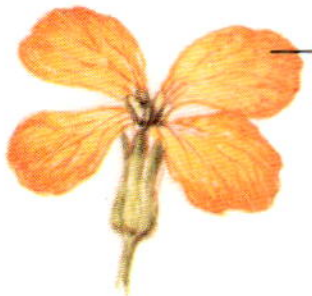

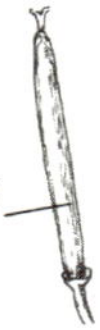

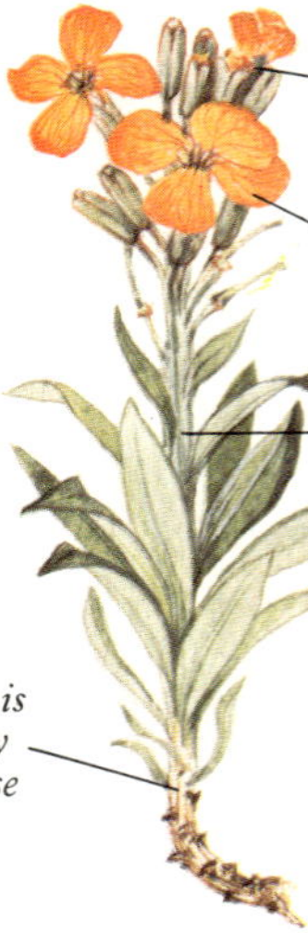

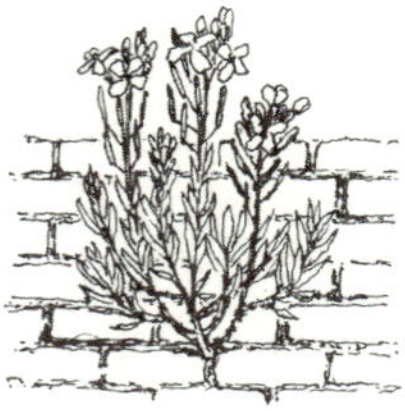

Plant becomes very woody with many stems

Wallflower

Cheiranthus cheiri
Habitat: Walls, rocks, waste ground, gardens.
Flowers: March to June. Perennial.
Distribution: Scattered throughout the British Isles; absent from the Scottish Highlands and the far north.

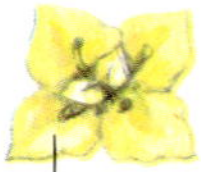

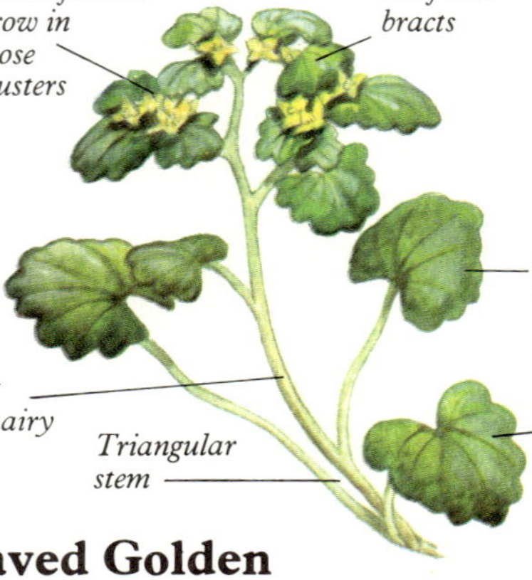

Do not confuse with *Opposite-leaved Golden Saxifrage* which has opposite leaves on a creeping, mat-forming stem.

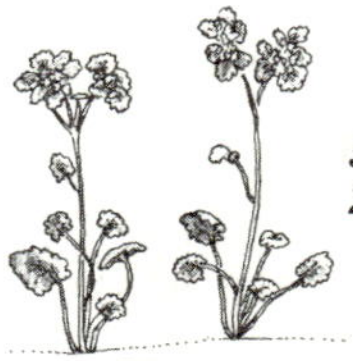

More or less upright

Alternate-leaved Golden Saxifrage

Chrysosplenium alternifolium
Habitat: Stream sides, wet rocks; damp, shady places.
Flowers: March to July. Perennial.
Distribution: Widespread but local throughout most of Britain; absent from Ireland.

YELLOW **4 PETALS**

Short, crowded flower spikes lengthen in fruit

3-6mm
0.2-0.3"

Fruits lie flat to branch

Flowers are pale yellow

Do not confuse with *Black Mustard* which has leaves that differ as shown:

Seed pod

Branches are always at wide angles to stem

1-2cm
0.4-0.8"

Stem leaves have 2 distinct basal lobes

Basal leaves have deep, toothed lobes

30-90cm
12-36"

Hedge Mustard

Sisymbrium officinale
Habitat: Roadsides, waste ground, cultivated land.
Flowers: May to August. Annual.
Distribution: Common in most of the British Isles.

Can become bushy with age

20-30mm
0.8-1.2"

Flowers grow in loose clusters

Flowers can be yellow, lilac or white

Petals usually have darker veins

Lower leaves have many toothed lobes

'Beak' at end of pod

2-10cm
0.8-4"

Seed pods look like beads strung together

Stem and leaves are bristly, often grey-green

Wild Radish

Raphanus raphanistrum
Also called: White Charlock, Runch, Cadlock.
Habitat: Roadsides, waste ground, cultivated land.
Flowers: May to September. Annual.
Distribution: Common throughout the British Isles.

20-80cm
8-32"

Plant branches from low down

YELLOW 4 PETALS

3-6mm
0.1-0.2"

Petals are twice as long as sepals

Distinctive fruits hang down

Flowers are in clusters at ends of branches

Stems are often purplish

Upper leaves are hairless, lower leaves downy

1-2.5cm
0.4-1"

Fruits become purplish black

Stem leaves clasp stem

0.5-1.2m
1'8"-4'

Woad

Isatis tinctoria
Habitat: Cornfields, cliffs, dry places.
Flowers: June to August. Biennial or perennial.
Distribution: Locally scattered throughout southern and central England; rare elsewhere.

Long, slender, leafy stems are branched at top

20-25mm
0.8-1"

Flowers grow in clusters

Fruiting stems lengthen behind flower cluster

Buds are above open flowers

Sepals spread out

Upper leaves are narrow and clasp stem

'Beak' at end of pod

4-11cm
1.6-4.4"

Seed pod

Leaves have wavy edges

Lower leaves are stalked and lobed with few bristles

0.6-1.2m
2-4'

Rape

Brassica napus
Also called: Cole, Swede.
Habitat: Roadsides, fields, motorways.
Flowers: April to August. Annual or biennial.
Distribution: Scattered throughout the British Isles.

Single stem is branched and can look bushy

YELLOW **4 PETALS**

- 4 greenish-yellow hairy sepals
- 4 bright yellow petals
- 20-25mm 0.8-1"
- Flowers grow in clusters of 2-8
- Many stamens; long style
- End leaflet has 3 lobes
- Leaves have 5-7 leaflets
- Brittle stems are grey-green and hairy
- Long, narrow fruit
- 30-90cm 12-36"

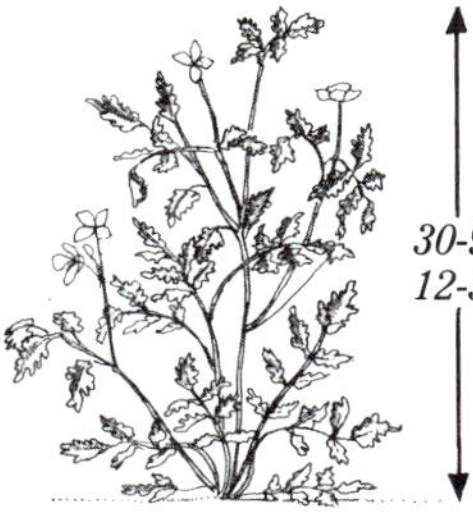

Greater Celandine

Chelidonium majus
Habitat: Hedgerows, walls, waste ground.
Flowers: May to September. Perennial.
Distribution: Common throughout the British Isles.

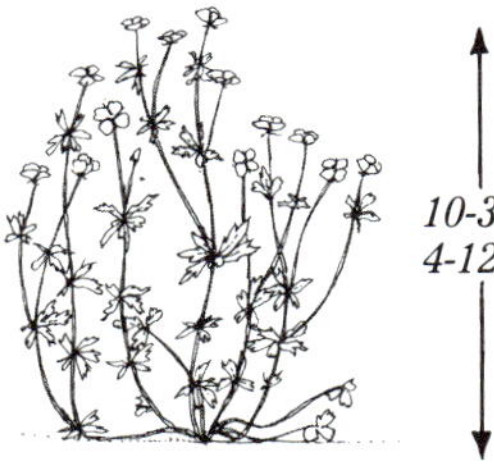

Plant has a bushy appearance

- 7-15mm 0.3-0.6"
- 4 petals
- Many flowers are in loose heads
- Stem leaves have 3 toothed lobes
- 4 inner and 4 outer sepals
- Short, downy flowering stem
- 2 toothed stipules look like leaves
- 10-30cm 4-12"

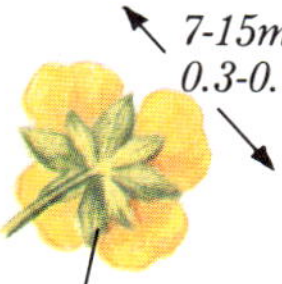

Tormentil

Potentilla erecta
Habitat: Grassland, mountains, heaths, bogs, moors.
Flowers: May to September. Perennial.
Distribution: Common throughout the British Isles.

Slender, trailing stems

YELLOW 5 PETALS

- 5 inner sepals
- 5 outer sepals
- 15-25mm / 0.6-1"
- Solitary flowers are on long, slender stalks
- Long, creeping stem roots at nodes
- Occasionally has 3, 4 or 7 leaflets
- Leaves are stalked, and usually have 5 toothed lobes
- Stipules may be toothed
- A low, downy plant
- New plants are produced at rooting nodes

Creeping Cinquefoil

Potentilla reptans
Habitat: Hedgebanks, waste places, grassland.
Flowers: June to September. Perennial.
Distribution: Common throughout the British Isles.

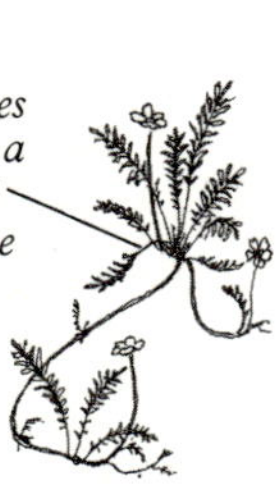

Creeping stems to 1m/3' long

- 15-25mm / 0.6-1"
- Solitary flowers
- Inner sepals are oval
- Leaflets are silvery underneath and sometimes also above
- Soft, silky leaves have 7-12 pairs of leaflets
- Tiny, intermediate leaflets
- Outer sepals are often toothed
- Flowering stalks and runners are often reddish
- Leaves form a basal rosette
- 5-15cm / 2-6"

Silverweed

Potentilla anserina
Habitat: Damp, grassy areas, waste ground, dunes.
Flowers: June to August. Perennial.
Distribution: Common throughout the British Isles.

New plants are formed where creeping stem roots

YELLOW **5 PETALS**

Yellow Pimpernel
Lysimachia nemorum
Habitat: Woods, shady hedgebanks, damp places.
Flowers: May to September. Perennial.
Distribution: Common throughout the British Isles.

Stems lie along the ground

Creeping Jenny
Lysimachia nummularia
Also called: Moneywort, Pennywort.
Habitat: Damp meadows, woods, grassy, shady places.
Flowers: June to August. Perennial.
Distribution: Common throughout the British Isles.

Creeping, mat forming stem

YELLOW 5 PETALS

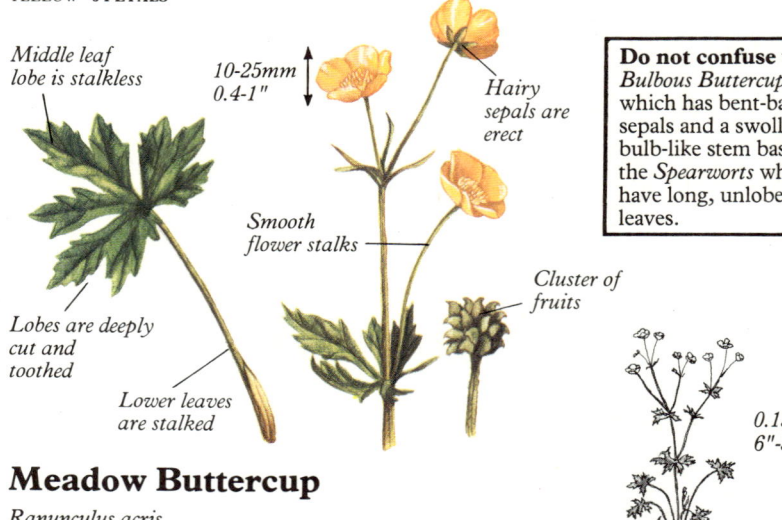

Meadow Buttercup

Ranunculus acris
Habitat: Grassland, damp meadows, gardens.
Flowers: April to October. Perennial.
Distribution: Common throughout the British Isles.

Stems are erect and hairy with many branches

Creeping Buttercup

Ranunculus repens
Habitat: Damp meadows, woods, gardens, grassland.
Flowers: May to September. Perennial.
Distribution: Common throughout the British Isles.

Stems that root at leaf nodes are often hidden in grass

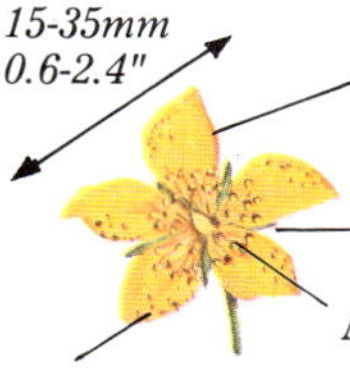

YELLOW **5 PETALS**

15-35mm
0.6-2.4"

5 petals

5 short sepals

Many stamens

Petals have black dots

2 raised lines run along the length of the stem

Flowers grow in small clusters

Leaves have semi-transparent dots

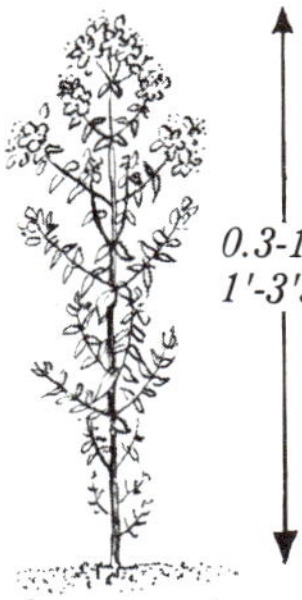

0.3-1m
1'-3'3"

Plant has many branches from a single stem

Common St. John's Wort

Hypericum perforatum
Also called: Perforate St. John's Wort, Rosin Rose.
Habitat: Hedgebanks, open woods, grassy areas.
Flowers: June to September. Perennial.
Distribution: Common throughout the British Isles except in central and northern Scotland.

10-20mm
0.4-0.8"

Cluster of fruits

Each fruit has a long purplish hook

Stipules are large, toothed and leaf-like

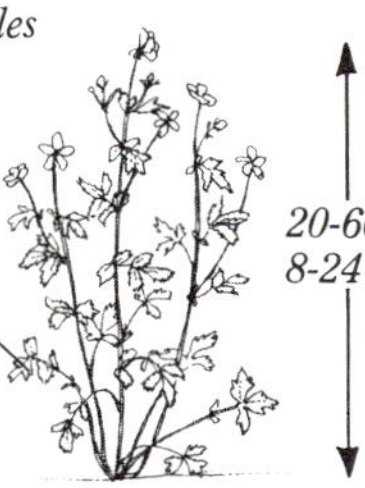

5 triangular sepals are as long as petals

Flowers are in open clusters

Upper leaves are unlobed

Plant is downy

Leaves at middle of stem have 3 toothed lobes

Stipules

Root leaves have 5-7 toothed leaflets

20-60cm
8-24"

Wood Avens

Geum urbanum
Also called: Herb Bennet, Yellow Strawberry.
Habitat: Woods, hedges, shady places.
Flowers: June to August. Perennial.
Distribution: Common throughout the British Isles.

Branched stems are upright

YELLOW 5 PETALS

Flowers grow in leafy, spiked clusters

Long leaves in whorls of 2-4

10-20mm 0.4-0.8"

Upper surfaces of leaves have tiny black or orange glands

Petals are often orange at base

Sepals have reddish edges

0.5-1.5m 1'8"-5'

Yellow Loosestrife

Lysimachia vulgaris
Habitat: By fresh water, ditches, moorlands.
Flowers: July to August. Perennial.
Distribution: Locally common throughout the British Isles except in the far north of Scotland.

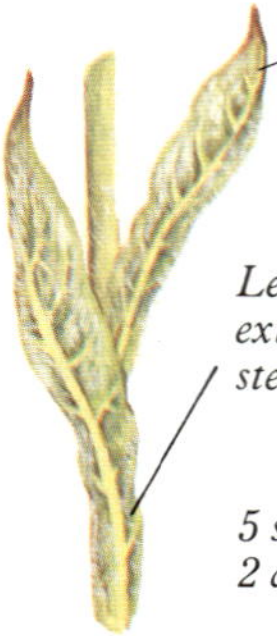

Plant is downy; stem has old leaf scars

Flowers grow in a long, dense spike

Hairs make plant look grey-green

Stem and flower spike are only rarely branched

Leaf bases extend down stem

15-30mm 0.6-1.2"

5 stamens: 3 are hairy, 2 are almost hairless

0.3-2m 1'-6'6"

Common Mullein

Verbascum thapsus
Also called: Aaron's Rod, Great Mullein.
Habitat: Sunny banks, waste places.
Flowers: June to August. Biennial.
Distribution: Common throughout the British Isles.

Robust plant is covered with whitish woolly hairs

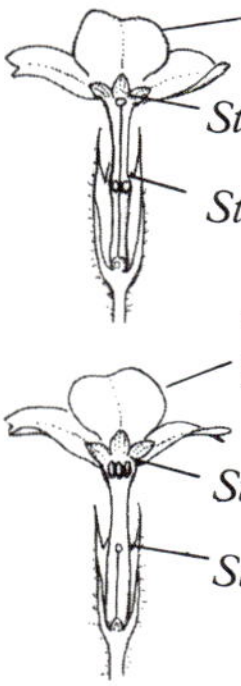

YELLOW **5 PETALS**

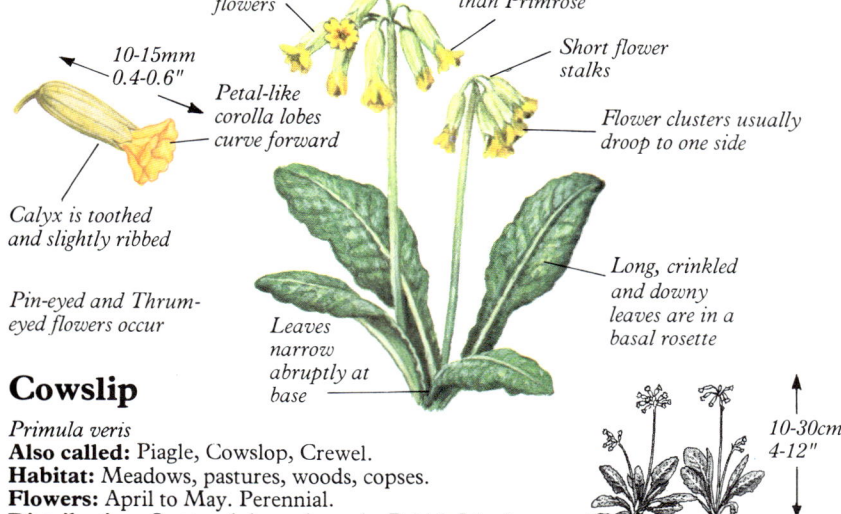

Two types of flower occur
Pin-eyed flower
Stigma
Stamens

Thrum-eyed flower
Stamens
Stigma

20-30mm
0.8-1.2"

Notched petals

Flowers are rarely pink or white

Single flowers are on long stalks

Downy, toothed and crinkled leaves are in a basal rosette

Leaves taper gradually to base

Primrose
Primula vulgaris
Habitat: Woods, hedges, open grassland.
Flowers: February to May. Perennial.
Distribution: Common throughout the British Isles.

10-20cm
4-8"

Forms small clumps with many flowers

Funnel-shaped flowers

Flowers are deeper yellow than Primrose

10-15mm
0.4-0.6"

Petal-like corolla lobes curve forward

Short flower stalks

Flower clusters usually droop to one side

Calyx is toothed and slightly ribbed

Pin-eyed and Thrum-eyed flowers occur

Long, crinkled and downy leaves are in a basal rosette

Leaves narrow abruptly at base

Cowslip
Primula veris
Also called: Piagle, Cowslop, Crewel.
Habitat: Meadows, pastures, woods, copses.
Flowers: April to May. Perennial.
Distribution: Scattered throughout the British Isles but mainly in the south; absent from much of Scotland.

10-30cm
4-12"

Often occurs in large numbers

YELLOW 5 PETALS

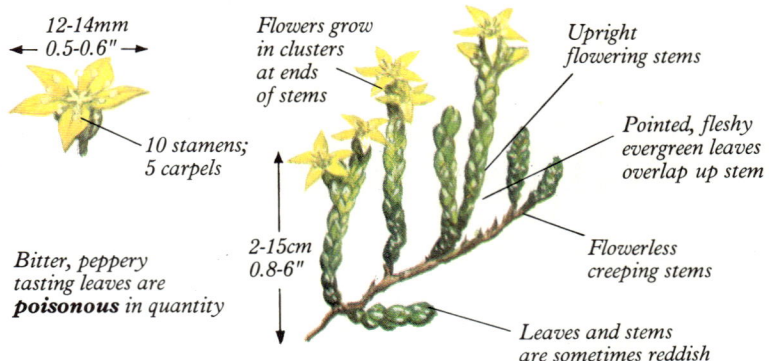

12-14mm
0.5-0.6"

Flowers grow in clusters at ends of stems

Upright flowering stems

10 stamens; 5 carpels

Pointed, fleshy evergreen leaves overlap up stem

2-15cm
0.8-6"

Flowerless creeping stems

Bitter, peppery tasting leaves are **poisonous** in quantity

Leaves and stems are sometimes reddish

Biting Stonecrop

Sedum acre
Also called: Wall Pepper, Yellow Stonecrop.
Habitat: Dry grassland, walls, shingle, dunes.
Flowers: June to July. Perennial.
Distribution: Common throughout most of the British Isles.

Forms very dense mats

20-25mm
0.8-1"

3 large sepals are distinctly veined

Flowers grow in loose, one-sided spike

5 petals

Leaves are in pairs

Leaves are narrow and oval, with white cottonish hairs underneath

Each leaf has 2 stipules at base

Stems are woody at base, often rooting at intervals

Common Rockrose

Helianthemum nummularium
Habitat: Grassland, scrub, well-drained soil.
Flowers: June to September. Perennial.
Distribution: Scattered throughout the British Isles except in Cornwall and north-west Scotland; rare in Ireland.

5-30cm
2-12"

A small, creeping undershrub

YELLOW **6 + PETALS**

35-60mm
1.4-2.4"

Papery bract

Trumpet is not longer than outer segments

6 wide-spreading petal-like segments

Flower stalk is flattened with 2 edges

Leaves are long, narrow, upright and often channelled

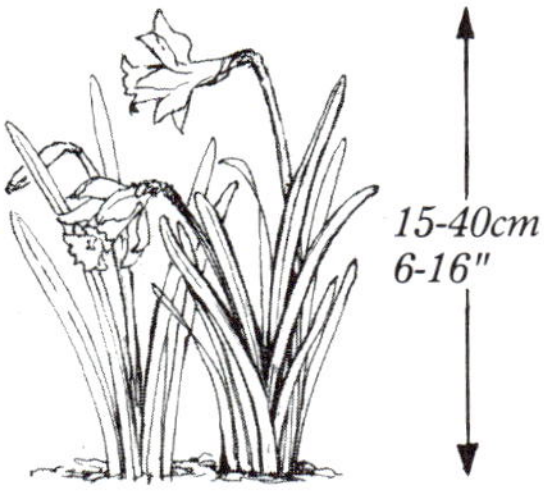

Wild Daffodil

Narcissus pseudonarcissus
Habitat: Woods, grassland, roadsides, riversides.
Flowers: February to April. Perennial.
Distribution: Local throughout the British Isles.

15-40cm
6-16"

Often occurs in large groups

Flowers are in a spike

12-15mm
0.5-0.6"

1 style, 6 orange anthers

6 petal-like segments

Stalk turns deep orange when fruits form

Stem leaves are short and sheathe stem

Root leaves are sword-shaped and often curved

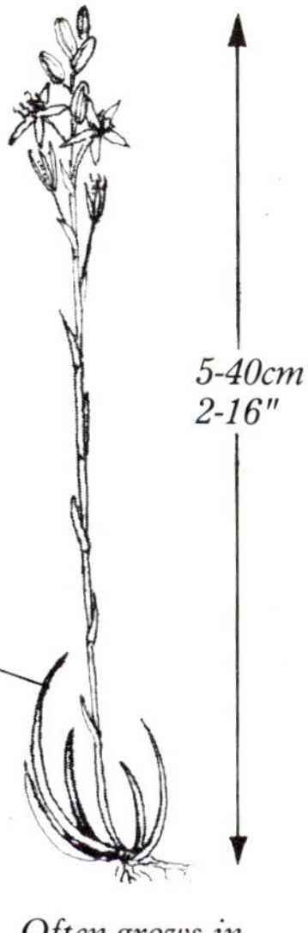

5-40cm
2-16"

Bog Asphodel

Narthecium ossifragum
Habitat: Wet heathland, boggy areas, wet, acid soil.
Flowers: July to September. Perennial.
Distribution: Scattered throughout the British Isles; more common in the West and North.

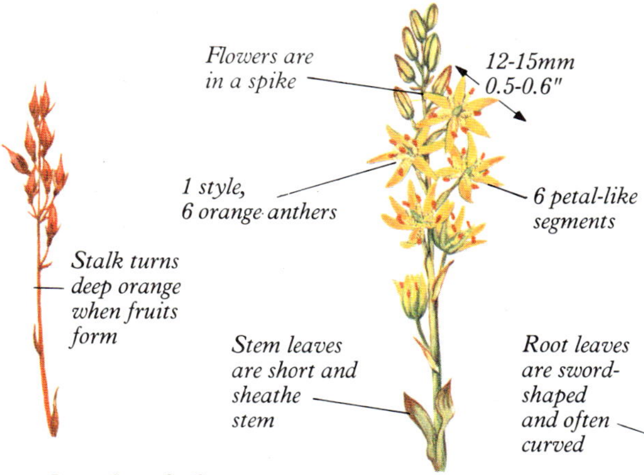

Often grows in large patches

YELLOW 6 + PETALS

8-12mm
0.3-0.5"

Long, red berries are edible

Leaves have toothed, bristly edges

Tufts of leaves

Grooved branches

Flowers, spines and leaves grow at intervals along the stem

Spines have 3 branches

Rounded flowers hang in clusters

1-3m
3'3"-9'9"

Barberry

Berberis vulgaris
Habitat: Hedges, light woodland.
Flowers: May to June. Perennial.
Distribution: Scattered throughout the British Isles.

A tall, often straggly, bushy shrub

5-8 petal-like sepals

Sepals are often greenish beneath

10-50mm
0.2-2"

Stout, hollow stem

Plant is hairless

Toothed leaves are often mottled above

Leaves are shiny, kidney- or heart-shaped and dark green

Lower leaves are stalked

15-45cm
6-18"

Marsh Marigold

Caltha palustris
Also called: King Cup, May Blobs, Gowland.
Habitat: Ditches, wet meadows, shady places.
Flowers: March to July. Perennial.
Distribution: Common throughout the British Isles.

Stems are usually erect; an upright, bushy plant

YELLOW 6+ PETALS

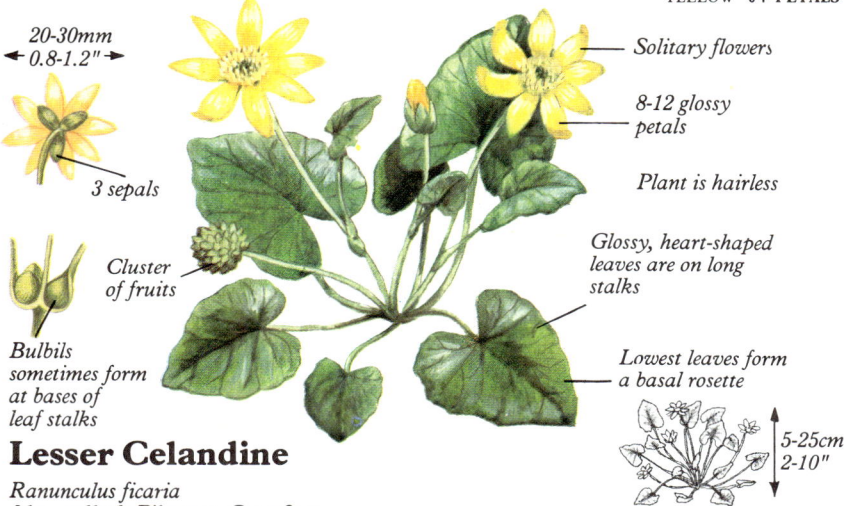

Lesser Celandine

Ranunculus ficaria
Also called: Pilewort, Crowfoot.
Habitat: Woods, grassy banks; damp, shady places.
Flowers: March to May. Perennial.
Distribution: Common throughout the British Isles.

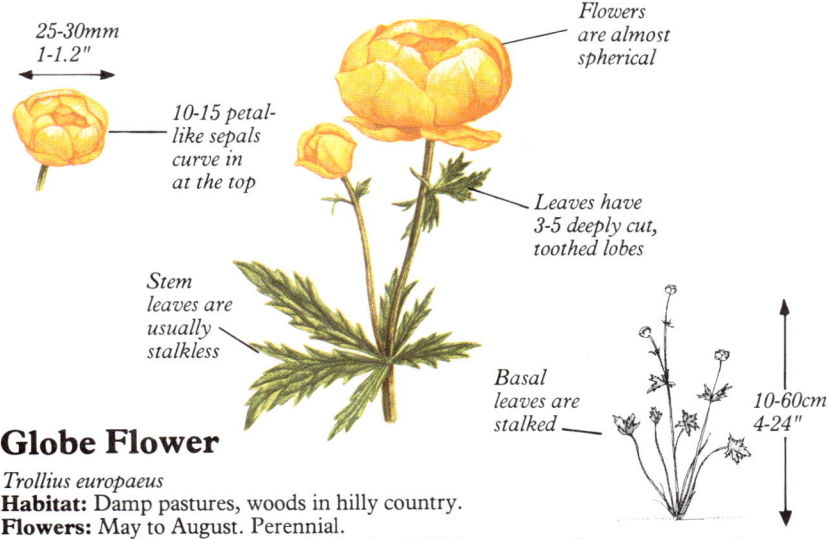

Globe Flower

Trollius europaeus
Habitat: Damp pastures, woods in hilly country.
Flowers: May to August. Perennial.
Distribution: Locally common in Scotland, Wales, northern England and Ireland; absent elsewhere.

111

YELLOW 6 + PETALS/COMPOSITE

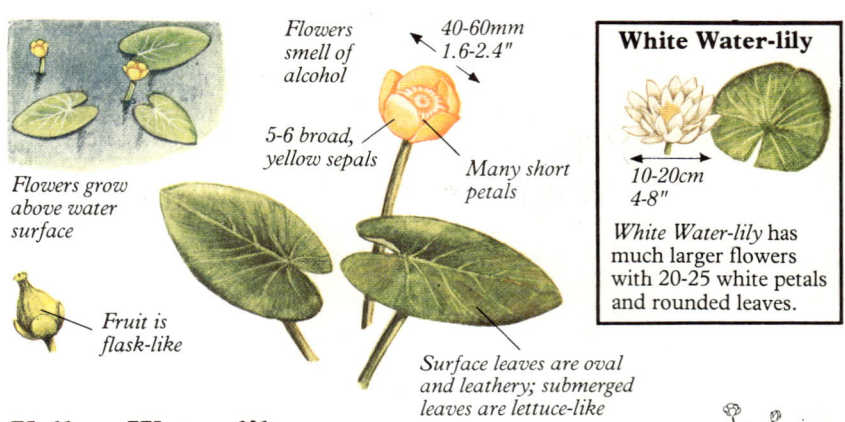

Yellow Water-lily

Nuphar lutea
Also called: Brandy Bottle, Waterblobs.
Habitat: Still and slow-moving water.
Flowers: June to September. Perennial.
Distribution: Common throughout the British Isles.

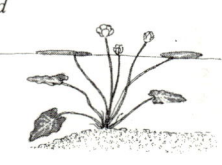

Stems to 3m/10'

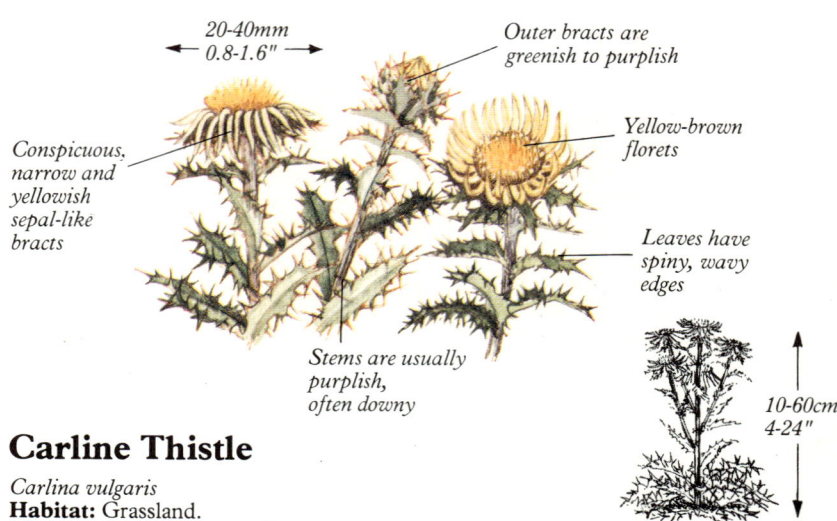

Carline Thistle

Carlina vulgaris
Habitat: Grassland.
Flowers: July to October. Biennial.
Distribution: Common throughout much of England, Wales and Ireland; absent from most of Scotland.

Dead flowers last through winter

YELLOW **COMPOSITE**

Do not confuse with *Common Groundsel* which has black-tipped outer bracts and no ray florets, or *Sticky Groundsel* which is sticky and greyish.

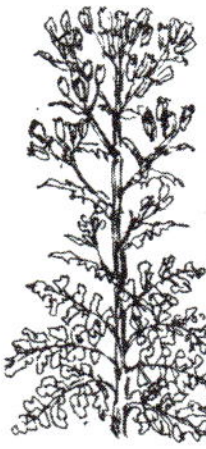

Flowerheads are in flat-topped clusters

Outer ray florets are curled back

7-10mm
0.3-0.4"

Bracts have sticky hairs

Narrow leaves have unequal, toothed lobes

Plant is downy

Stem is thin and furrowed

15-70cm
6-28"

Wood Groundsel

Senecio sylvaticus
Also called: Heath Groundsel.
Habitat: Heathland, open woodland, sandy soils.
Flowers: July to September. Annual.
Distribution: Locally common throughout the British Isles except in the Outer Hebrides and Shetland.

Upright plant branches from a single stem

Triangular end lobe

Seeds' hairy parachutes form the dandelion 'clock'

Ray florets only

30-60mm
1.2-2.4"

Bud

Outer bracts curl down

Leaf shape is variable

Lobes are sometimes toothed

Stems are hollow, sometimes reddish and downy

Dandelion

Taraxacum vulgare
Also called: Piss-a-bed, Clock Flower, Clock.
Habitat: Open ground, fields, walls, gardens, lawns.
Flowers: March to November. Perennial.
Distribution: Common throughout the British Isles.

15-30cm
6-12"

Rarely grows singly; leaves form a basal rosette

YELLOW **COMPOSITE**

Stalk is thickest below flowerhead

Solitary, daisy-like flowers

Green bracts have brown edges

35-60mm 1.4-2.4"

Lower leaves are lobed and stalked

Disc florets and ray florets are golden yellow

Upper leaves are toothed and clasp stem

20-50cm 8-20"

Corn Marigold

Chrysanthemum segetum
Habitat: Cultivated and disturbed ground, banks.
Flowers: June to September. Annual.
Distribution: Fairly common throughout the British Isles.

Usually forms brilliant yellow patches

Fruiting head; the seeds have white parachutes

Outer female florets have brighter yellow rays

15-35mm 0.6-1.4"

Orange-yellow male disc florets

Green bracts

10-25cm 4-10"

Whitish flowering stems have usually purplish scales

Leaves are woolly and whitish underneath

Occasionally small leaves appear at flowering time

Leaves appear after the flowers

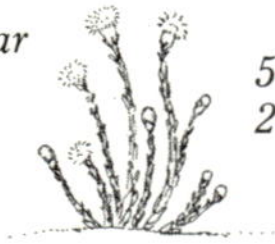

5-15cm 2-6"

Coltsfoot

Tussilago farfara
Habitat: Cultivated and waste land, waysides, paths.
Flowers: February to April. Perennial.
Distribution: Common throughout the British Isles.

Many flowers together; one of the first of the year

YELLOW **COMPOSITE**

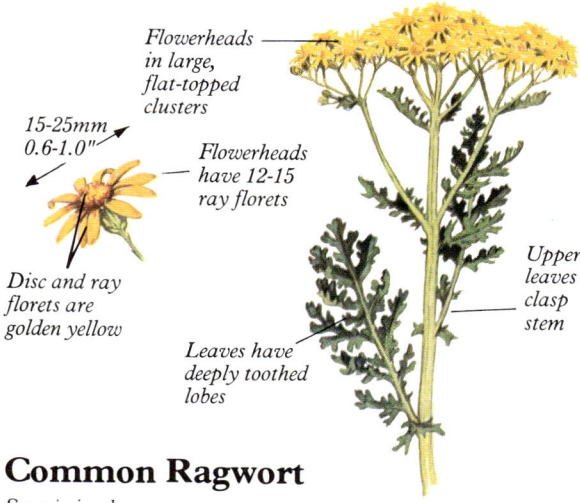

Flowerheads in large, flat-topped clusters

15-25mm
0.6-1.0"

Flowerheads have 12-15 ray florets

Disc and ray florets are golden yellow

Upper leaves clasp stem

Leaves have deeply toothed lobes

Common Ragwort
Senecio jacobea
Habitat: Waste ground, roadsides, neglected pasture.
Flowers: June to October. Biennial or perennial.
Distribution: Common throughout the British Isles.

Do not confuse with other *Ragworts* and *Groundsels* which differ in size, leaf and form of flowerhead.

Often has black and yellow Cinnabar Moth caterpillars on it

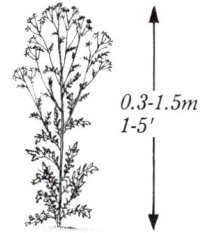

0.3-1.5m
1-5'

Upright, stately, normally hairless plant

Flowerheads are waisted

20-25mm
0.8-1"

All florets are rayed

Lower leaves are lobed with winged stalks

Lobes at leaf bases spread outwards

Outer florets are often purplish beneath

Leaves have pointed teeth but no prickles

Stem leaves are stalkless

Common Sowthistle
Sonchus oleraceus
Habitat: Cultivated land, roadsides, waste places.
Flowers: June to October. Annual.
Distribution: Common throughout the British Isles.

Do not confuse with *Prickly Sowthistle* which has spiny, prickly leaves with basal lobes that clasp the stem.

0.2-1.5m
8"-5'

Upright, usually untidy looking.

YELLOW **COMPOSITE**

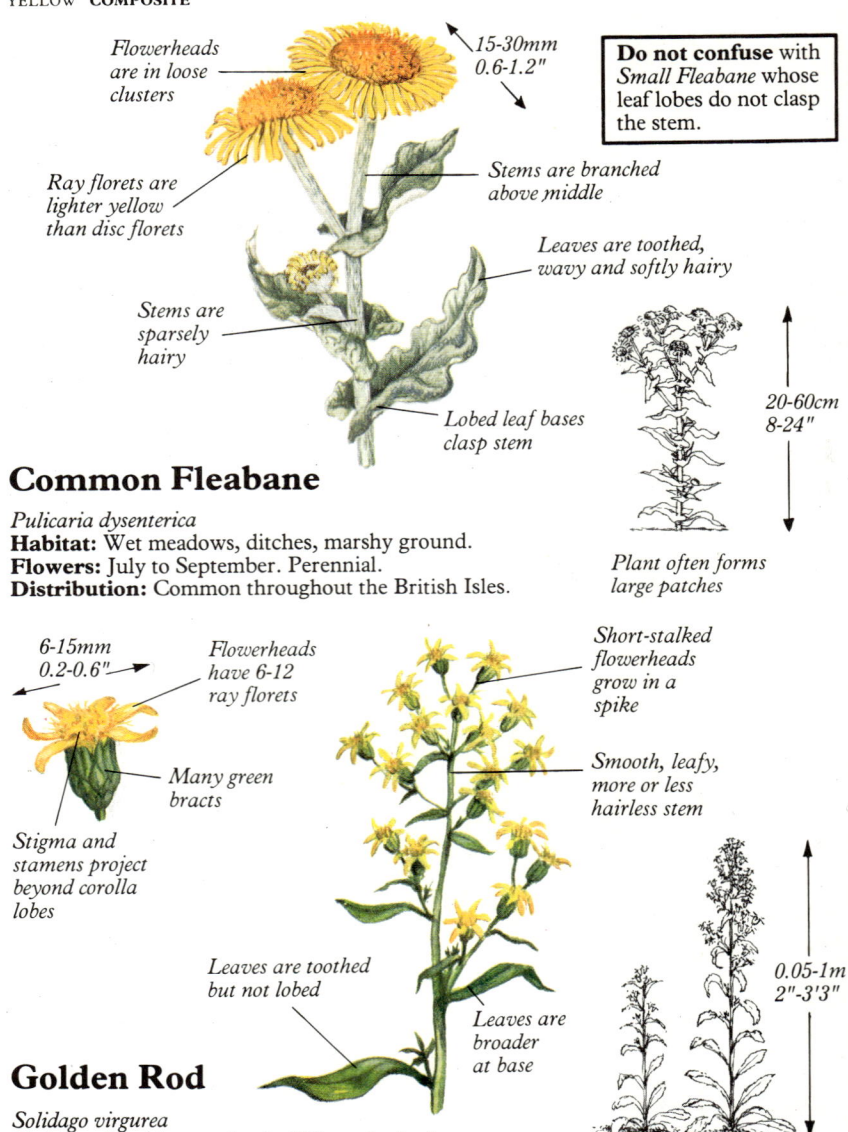

Flowerheads are in loose clusters

15-30mm 0.6-1.2"

Do not confuse with *Small Fleabane* whose leaf lobes do not clasp the stem.

Ray florets are lighter yellow than disc florets

Stems are branched above middle

Leaves are toothed, wavy and softly hairy

Stems are sparsely hairy

Lobed leaf bases clasp stem

20-60cm 8-24"

Common Fleabane

Pulicaria dysenterica
Habitat: Wet meadows, ditches, marshy ground.
Flowers: July to September. Perennial.
Distribution: Common throughout the British Isles.

Plant often forms large patches

6-15mm 0.2-0.6"

Flowerheads have 6-12 ray florets

Short-stalked flowerheads grow in a spike

Many green bracts

Smooth, leafy, more or less hairless stem

Stigma and stamens project beyond corolla lobes

Leaves are toothed but not lobed

Leaves are broader at base

0.05-1m 2"-3'3"

Golden Rod

Solidago virgurea
Habitat: Woods, grassland, cliffs, rocks, hedges.
Flowers: July to September. Perennial.
Distribution: Common throughout the British Isles but rarer in south-east England.

Single, occasionally branched stems; plant is very variable

YELLOW **LIPPED**

Honeysuckle

Lonicera periclymenum
Also called: Woodbine, Woodbind.
Habitat: Woods, hedges, scrubland, gardens.
Flowers: June to September. Perennial.
Distribution: Common throughout the British Isles.

Common Cow Wheat

Melampyrum pratense
Habitat: Grassland, heaths, woods.
Flowers: May to September. Annual.
Distribution: Common throughout the British Isles.

YELLOW **LIPPED**

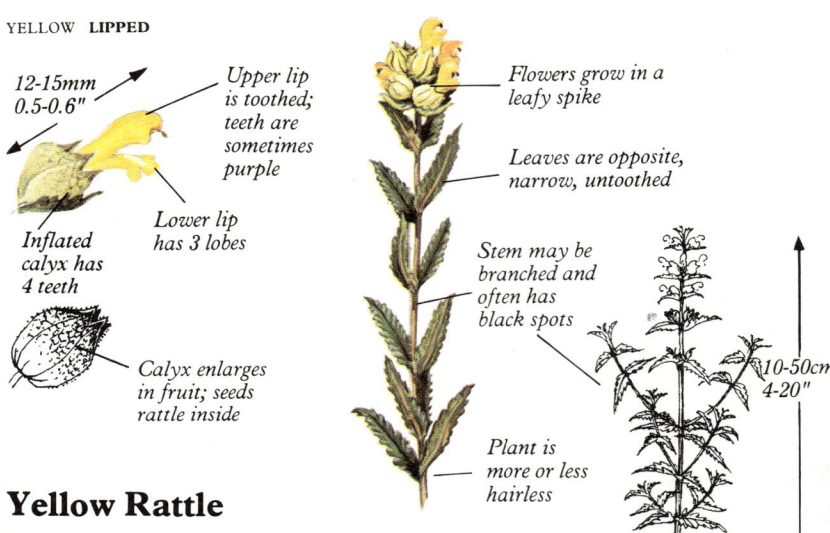

12-15mm
0.5-0.6"

Upper lip is toothed; teeth are sometimes purple

Lower lip has 3 lobes

Inflated calyx has 4 teeth

Calyx enlarges in fruit; seeds rattle inside

Flowers grow in a leafy spike

Leaves are opposite, narrow, untoothed

Stem may be branched and often has black spots

Plant is more or less hairless

10-50cm
4-20"

Yellow Rattle

Rhinanthus minor
Habitat: Grassy areas, cornfields.
Flowers: May to September. Annual.
Distribution: Common throughout the British Isles.

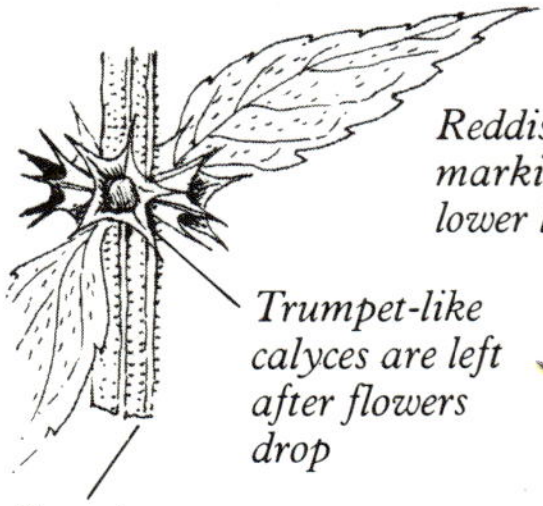

Usually occurs in quantity in grass

Reddish-brown markings on lower lip

Trumpet-like calyces are left after flowers drop

Stem is square and hairy

Hairy leaves are in opposite pairs

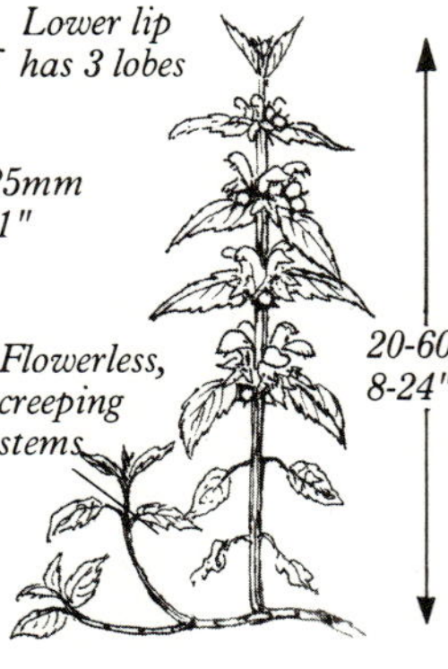

Flowers are in whorls at bases of upper leaves

Top of upper lip is hairy

Lower lip has 3 lobes

20-25mm
0.8-1"

Flowerless, creeping stems

20-60cm
8-24"

Yellow Archangel

Lamiastrum galeobdolon
Also called: Yellow Dead-nettle, Weasel's Snout.
Habitat: Woods, wood edges, copses, gardens.
Flowers: May to June. Perennial.
Distribution: Common in southern and central England but rarer elsewhere; absent from much of Scotland.

Forms fair-sized patches

YELLOW SPURRED

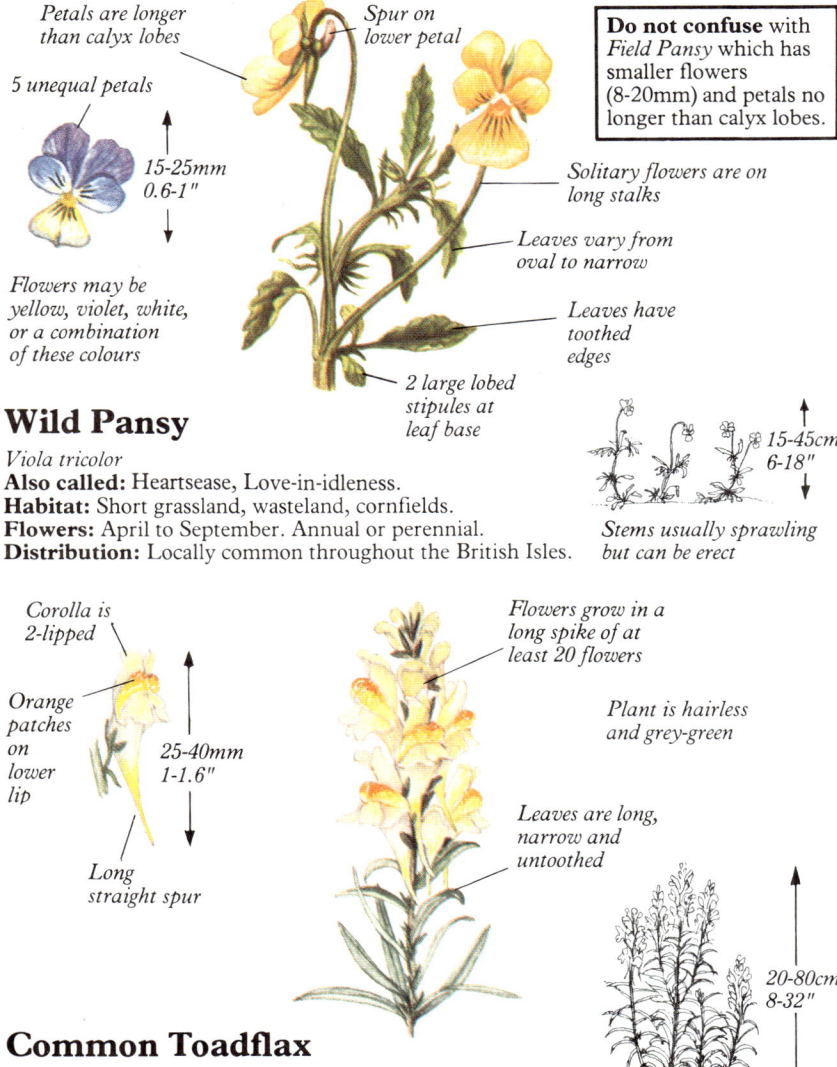

Petals are longer than calyx lobes

5 unequal petals

15-25mm 0.6-1"

Flowers may be yellow, violet, white, or a combination of these colours

Spur on lower petal

Do not confuse with *Field Pansy* which has smaller flowers (8-20mm) and petals no longer than calyx lobes.

Solitary flowers are on long stalks

Leaves vary from oval to narrow

Leaves have toothed edges

2 large lobed stipules at leaf base

15-45cm 6-18"

Wild Pansy
Viola tricolor
Also called: Heartsease, Love-in-idleness.
Habitat: Short grassland, wasteland, cornfields.
Flowers: April to September. Annual or perennial.
Distribution: Locally common throughout the British Isles.

Stems usually sprawling but can be erect

Corolla is 2-lipped

Orange patches on lower lip

25-40mm 1-1.6"

Long straight spur

Flowers grow in a long spike of at least 20 flowers

Plant is hairless and grey-green

Leaves are long, narrow and untoothed

20-80cm 8-32"

Common Toadflax
Linaria vulgaris
Habitat: Waste ground, grassland, banks, gardens.
Flowers: June to October. Perennial.
Distribution: Common throughout England and Wales; less common in Ireland; absent from northern Scotland.

Many very leafy stems are branched at top

YELLOW **PEA**

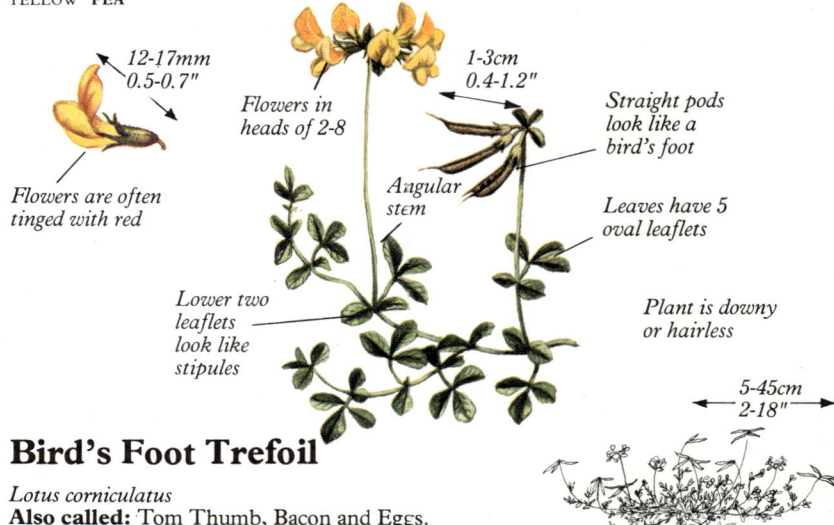

Bird's Foot Trefoil

Lotus corniculatus
Also called: Tom Thumb, Bacon and Eggs.
Habitat: Grassland, roadsides, lawns.
Flowers: May to September. Perennial.
Distribution: Common throughout the British Isles.

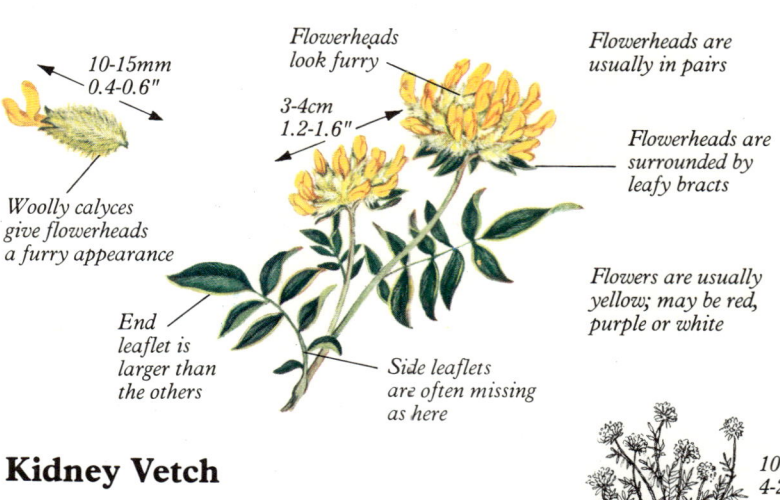

Kidney Vetch

Anthyllis vulneraria
Also called: Lady's Fingers, Lamb's Toes.
Habitat: Dry grassland.
Flowers: April to September. Perennial.
Distribution: Scattered throughout the British Isles.

YELLOW **PEA**

Calyx has upright hairs

15-25mm 0.6-1"

Flowers smell of coconut

Flowers grow from leaf nodes

Plant is a spiny shrub

Branched spines are long, hard and deeply furrowed.

Main branches are upright

0.3-1.2m 1-4'

Gorse

Ulex europaeus
Also called: Furze, Whin, French-Fuzz.
Habitat: Heaths and open, grassy places.
Flowers: All year, but best March to June. Perennial.
Distribution: Fairly common throughout the British Isles except in northern Scotland and western Ireland.

Often many bushes cover a large area

Calyx is hairless

Flowers grow from leaf nodes

Pod is black with brown hairs

15-25mm 0.6-1"

Do not confuse with *Spanish Broom* which has rounded, not angled stems and long narrow leaves without leaflets.

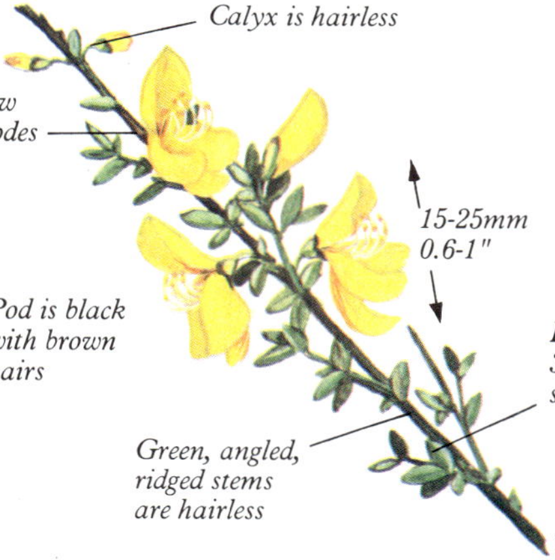

Leaves usually have 3 leaflets but are sometimes single

Green, angled, ridged stems are hairless

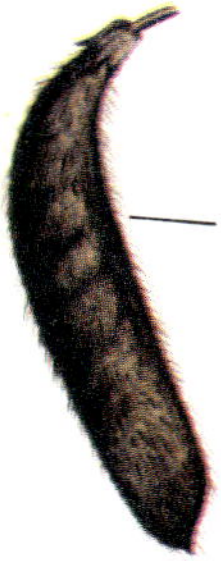

Broom

Cytisus scoparius
Habitat: Heaths, open woods, waste and scrubland.
Flowers: May to June. Perennial.
Distribution: Locally common throughout the British Isles except in Orkney and Shetland.

50-200cm 20-80"

Upright, well branched; often forms a large bush

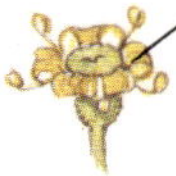

YELLOW **UMBELLIFER**
BROWN **6+ PETALS**

2mm / 0.1"
Tiny flowers have curved petals

Flowers grow in umbrella-shaped clusters in flat-topped heads

Narrow wings

Fruit is a flattened egg shape

3-10cm / 1.2-4"

Leaflets are deeply toothed

Distinctive leaves have leaflets in 2 rows

Hollowed, furrowed, hairy stems

0.3-1.5m / 1-5'

Wild Parsnip

Pastinaca sativa
Habitat: Roadsides, waste ground, grassy places.
Flowers: July to August. Perennial.
Distribution: Scattered throughout England and Wales, especially in the south-east; rarer in Scotland and Ireland.

A tall, branched, stately plant

3-4mm / 0.1-0.2"

Stem continues above flowers

3 petal-like inner segments

Flowers grow in much branched clusters

3 petal-like outer segments

Small flowers

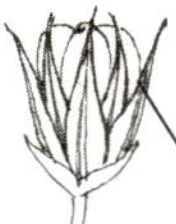

Stiff stems vary in colour from green to yellowish green

Fruit

Reddish to dark-brown sheaths at base

0.3-1.5m / 1-5'

Soft Rush

Juncus effusus
Habitat: Wet fields, boggy areas, by water.
Flowers: June to August. Perennial.
Distribution: Common throughout the British Isles.

Smooth, upright plant forms small, dense clusters

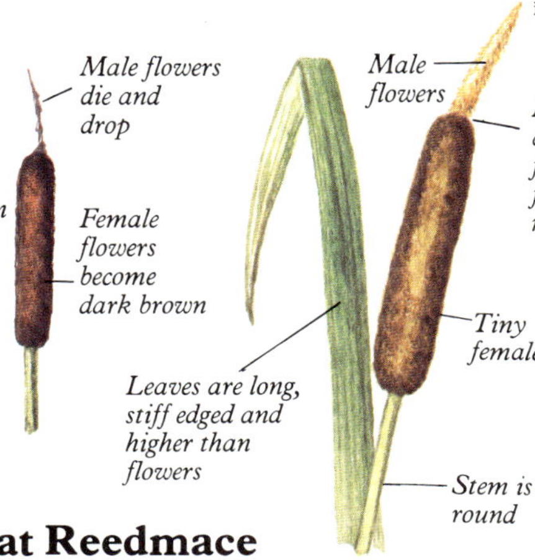

BROWN COMPOSITE/TUBULAR OR BELL

Male flowers die and drop

10-20cm
4-8"

Female flowers become dark brown

Male flowers

Male and female flowers meet

Leaves are long, stiff edged and higher than flowers

Tiny female flowers

Stem is round

Do not confuse with *Lesser Reedmace* on which the male and female flowers are separated.

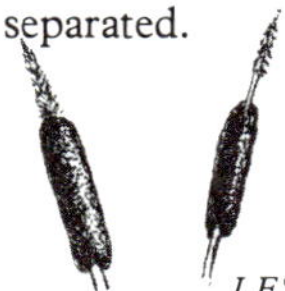

GREAT REEDMACE   LESSER REEDMACE

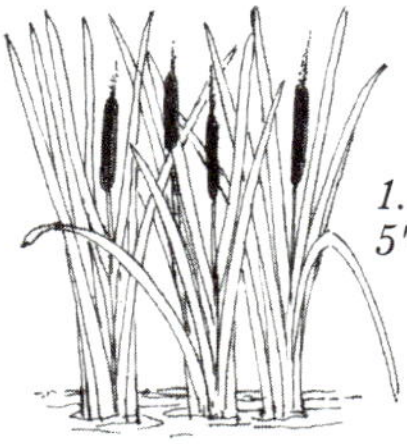

Great Reedmace

Typha latifolia
Also called: Bulrush, False Bulrush, Cat's-tail.
Habitat: Slow-moving or still water.
Flowers: June to July. Perennial.
Distribution: Common in England and Ireland; local in Wales and southern Scotland; rare northwards.

1.5m-2.5m
5'-8.3'

Plant forms large colonies in shallow water

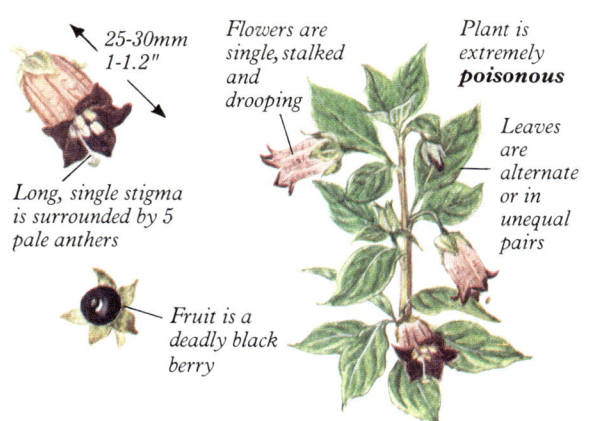

25-30mm
1-1.2"

Flowers are single, stalked and drooping

Plant is extremely **poisonous**

Leaves are alternate or in unequal pairs

Long, single stigma is surrounded by 5 pale anthers

Fruit is a deadly black berry

Woody Nightshade (Bittersweet)

Woody Nightshade (Bittersweet) has these purple and yellow flowers in stalked clusters, leaves that are usually lobed and red berries. **Poisonous.**

Deadly Nightshade

Atropa belladonna
Also called: Dwale, Belladonna, Devil's Cherries.
Habitat: Woods, scrub, rocky places, old ruins.
Flowers: June to August. Perennial.
Distribution: Local throughout the British Isles.

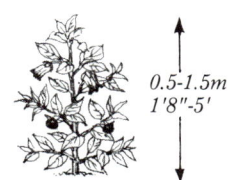

0.5-1.5m
1'8"-5'

Usually well branched

Further Reading

The Alpine Flowers of Britain and Europe. C. Grey-Wilson, M. Blamey (Collins 1979)

Atlas of British Flora. Ed. F.H. Perring and S.M. Walters (E.P. Publishing 1976)

An Atlas of the Wild Flowers of Britain and Northern Europe. Alistair Fitter (Collins 1978)

Collins Pocket Guide to Wild Flowers. D. McClintock and R.S.R. Fitter (Collins 1956)

The Concise British Flora in Colour. W. Keble Martin (Ebury Press/Michael Joseph 1969)

The Concise Flowers of Europe. O. Polunin (Oxford University Press 1972)

Drawings of British Plants. Stella Ross-Craig (Bell and Hyman 1979)

The Englishman's Flora. G. Grigson (Paladin 1975)

Excursion Flora. A.R. Clapham, T.G. Tutin and E.F. Warburg (Cambridge University Press 1968)

A Field Guide in Colour to Wild Flowers. D. Aichele and M. Golte-Bechtle (Octopus 1975)

Flora Europaea. Vols 1-5. Ed. T.G. Tutin, H.V. Heywood, N.A. Burges, D.H. Valentine, S.M. Walters and D.A. Webb (Cambridge University Press 1968-1980)

Flora of the British Isles. A.R. Clapham, T.G. Tutin and E.F. Warburg (Cambridge University Press 1952)

A Guide to Wild Plants. Michael Jordan (Millington 1976)

Poisonous Plants and Fungi. Pamela North (Blandford 1967)

Wild Flowers of Britain. Roger Phillips (Pan 1977)

The Wild Flowers of Britain and Northern Europe. R. Fitter, A. Fitter, M. Blamey (Collins 1974)

Wild Plants and the Law

Many European plants have been brought to the edge of extinction, due to the destruction of their natural habitat and over-collection. The Conservation of Wild Creatures and Wild Plants Act, 1975, was passed to try and control the collection of rare species. Under the terms of the Act it is illegal for any wild plant to be uprooted "without landowner's permission". There is, in addition, a list of twenty-one species which are so rare that it is illegal to damage or take away any part of the plant. These plants are:

Alpine Gentian	**Ghost Orchid**	**Red Helleborine**
Alpine Sow-thistle	**Killarney Fern**	**Snowdon Lily**
Alpine Woodsia	**Lady's Slipper**	**Spiked Speedwell**
Blue Heath	**Mezereon**	**Spring Gentian**
Cheddar Pink	**Military Orchid**	**Teesdale Sandwort**
Diapensia	**Monkey Orchid**	**Tufted Saxifrage**
Drooping Saxifrage	**Oblong Woodsia**	**Wild Gladiolus**

Cheddar Pink, Red Helleborine and Spring Gentian are illustrated in this book.

Index of English Names

Page numbers referring to illustrations appear in **bold type**

Aaron's Rod **106**
Adder's Meat **63**
Alfalfa **42**
Alkanet, Evergreen 43
All-good **86**
Alpine Rock Cress **61**
Anemone, Wood **72**
  Yellow Wood 72
Angel Flower **76**
Apple Pie **14**
Arabis, Garden 61
Arum, Wild **88**
Avens, Water **20**
  Wood **105**

Bachelor's Buttons **39**
Bacon and Eggs **120**
Balsam, Himalayan **31**
  Indian **31**
  Orange 31
  Touch-me-not 31
  Wild 31
Barberry **110**
Bartsia, Red **26**
Bats-in-the-belfry **55**
Bear's Foot **91**
Belladonna **123**
Bellbine **78**
Bellflowers 55
Betony **27**
Bilberry **12**
Billy's Button **20**
Bindweed, Black **92**
  Greater **78**
  Hedge **78**
Bird's Foot Trefoil **120**
Bishop's Weed **81**
Bistort **22**
  Alpine **70**
  Viviparous **70**
Bittersweet **123**
Blackberry **66**
Blaeberry **12**
Blawort **50**
Blue Aconite **47**
Bluebell **54**, **55**
Blue Bonnets **50**
Bluebottle **50**
Blue Bottle **54**
Blue Butcher **32**
Blue Endive **50**
Blue Rocket **47**
Bog Asphodel **109**
Borage **47**
Bouncing Bett **21**
Bramble **66**

Brandy Bottle **112**
Brier **66**
Brooklime **43**
Broom **121**
  Spanish 121
Brownwort **40**
Bryony, Black **90**
  Red **68**
  White **68**
Bugle, Common **51**, 52
Bugloss, Viper's **54**
Bulrush **123**
Bunch o' Daisies **76**
Bunks **50**
Burnet, Great **37**
Butterbur **25**
Buttercup, Bulbous 104
  Creeping **104**
  Meadow **104**
Butterwort, Common **40**
  Pale 40

Cadlock **99**
Campion, Bladder **62**
  Moss **19**
  Red **17**, 21
  White **62**
Candytuft, Wild **60**
Carrot, Wild **82**
Cat's-tail **123**
Celandine, Greater **101**
  Lesser **111**
Centaury, Common **18**
  Slender 18
Chamomile, Wild **75**
Charlock, White **99**
Cherry Pie **14**
Chickweed **64**
  Field Mouse-ear **63**
Chicory **50**
Cinquefoil, Creeping **102**
Clary, Meadow **53**
  Wild 53
Cleavers **59**
Climbing Buckwheat **92**
Clock **113**
Clock Flower **113**
Clover, Crimson **13**
  Dutch **79**
  Kentish **79**
  Red **13**
  White **79**
Cocks and Hens **93**
Codlins and Cream **14**
Cole **100**
Coltsfoot **114**

Columbine **56**
Comfrey, Common **53**
Convolvulus **78**
Cornbind **92**
Corn Cockle **17**
Cornflower **50**
Corn Spurrey **64**
Country Lawyers **66**
Cowslip **107**
Cowslop **107**
Cow Wheat, Common **117**
Cranesbill, Bloody **10**
  Meadow **45**
  Pyrenean 20
  Wood 45
Creeping Jenny **103**
Crewel **107**
Crow Flower **54**
Crowfoot **32**, **111**
  Water **65**
Cuckoo **32**
Cuckoo Flower **15**
Cuckoo Pint **88**
Cuckoo's Meat **8**

Daffodil, Wild **109**
Daisy **74**
  Horse **74**
  Michaelmas **48**
  Moon **74**
  Ox-eye **74**
Dandelion **113**
Deadmen's Bells **30**
Dead-nettle, Spotted **76**
  White **76**
  Yellow **118**
Devil's Bell **55**
Devil's Cherries **123**
Dock, Broad-leaved **89**
Dropwort 71
  Corky-fruited Water **82**
Dwale **123**
Dwarf Cornel **35**

Easter Ledges **22**
Elder, Ground **81**
Eyebright **77**

Fairy Gloves **30**
False Bulrush **123**
False Cleavers **59**
Fat Hen **85**
Fellon-grass **91**
Felonwort **68**
Feverfew **75**

Figwort, Common **40**
  Water 40
Fireweed **14**
Fleabane, Common **116**
  Small 116
Flowering Withy **14**
Forget-me-not, Common **46**
  Field **46**
Fox and Cubs **12**
Foxglove **30**
French-Fuzz **121**
French Lilac **33**
French Willow **14**
Fritillary **37**
Frog-bit **59**
Fumitory, Common **30**
  Ramping 30
  Small 30
  Wall 30
Furze **121**
  Needle 113

Garlic, Bear's **73**
  Crow **29**
  Hedge **60**
  Triangular-stalked **73**
  Wild **73**
Garlic Mustard **60**
Gentian, Alpine 45
  Spring **45**
Globe Flower **111**
Goat's Rue **33**
Golden Rod **116**
Good King Henry **86**
Goosegrass **59**
Gorse **121**
Goutweed **81**
Gowland **110**
Granny's Bonnet **20**
Granny's Nightcap **72**
Green Lily **91**
Green Sauce **8**
Gromwell, Blue **46**
  Purple **46**
Ground Ivy 51, **52**
Groundsel, Common 113
  Heath **113**
  Sticky **113**
  Wood **113**

Hadder **15**
Hardhead **39**
Hardheads **94**
Harebell **55**
Hawkweed, Orange **12**

125

Hayriff **59**
Healing Leaf **22**
Heartsease **119**
Heath **15**
  Cross-leaved 29
Heather **15**, 29
  Bell **29**
Hedder **15**
Hedgeheriff **59**
Hedge Mustard **99**
Hedge Pink **21**
Heliotrope, Winter 25
Hellebore, Green **91**
  Stinking **91**
Helleborine, Dark Red 24
  Red **24**
Hemp Agrimony **25**
Hepatica **48**
Herb Bennet **105**
Herb Gerard **81**
Herb Paris **90**
Herb Robert **20**
Hogweed **81**
  Giant 81
Honeysuckle **117**
Hop **92**
Houndstongue, Common **10**
  Green 10
Huckleberry **12**
Hyacinth, Wild **54**

Iron Root **86**
Ironweed **39**

Jack-by-the-hedge **60**
Joy of the Mountain **28**

Keck **80, 81**
Kelk **80**
Kesh **81**
King Cup **110**
Knapweed, Lesser **39**
  Greater **39**
Knotgrass **23**

Lady's Fingers **120**
Lady's Lace **80**
Lady's Smock **15**
Lady's Thimble **55**
Lamb's Quarters **86**
Lamb's Toes **120**
Lap-love **92**
Larkspur **56**
  Eastern 56
  Forking 56
Latherwort **21**
Lavender, Lax-flowered Sea 36
  Sea **36**

Leek, Three-cornered **73**
Lily, Green **91**
Lily-of-the-Valley **78**
Ling **15**
Little Robin 20
Livelong **22**
London Basket **20**
Loosestrife, Purple **24**
  Yellow **106**
Lords and Ladies **88**
Love-in-idleness **119**
Lucerne 33, **42**

Maithen **75**
Mallow, Common **21**
  Marsh 21
  Musk 21
Mandrake **68**
Margeurite **74**
Marigold, Corn **114**
  Marsh **110**
Marjoram **28**
  Wild **28**
Masterwort, Great **79**
May Blobs **110**
Mayflower **15**
Mayweed, Rayless 75
  Scented **75**
Meadow Rue, Common **96**
Meadowsweet **71**
Melancholy Gentleman **79**
Meldweed **85**
Mercury **86**
  Annual 84
  Dog's **84**
Midsummer Men **22**
Milfoil **76**
Milk Maids **15**
Mints 28
Mistletoe **87**
Moneywort **103**
Monkshood **47**
Mountain Sanicle **79**
Muckweed **85**
Mullein, Common **106**
  Great **106**
Mustard, Black 99
  Garlic **60**
  Hedge **99**

Nemony **72**
Nettle **85**
Nettle-leaved Bellflower **55**
Nightshade, Black **68**
  Deadly **123**
  Garden **68**
  Green 68
  Woody **123**

Orache, Common **86**
Orchid, Bee **26**
  Common Spotted 32
  Early Purple **32**
  Fly 26
  Fragrant 32
  Lizard **95**
  Pyramidal **32**
  Scented 32
  Spider 26
Organy **28**
Orpine **22**

Pansy, Field 119
  Wild **119**
Parsley, Cow **80**
  Upright Hedge **80**
Parsnip Cow **81**
  Wild **122**
Pasque Flower **36**
Pea, Everlasting 34
  Narrow-leaved Everlasting **34**
  Wild **34**
Pellitory-of-the-wall **87**
Pennywort **103**
Periwinkle, Greater 44
  Lesser **44**
Pheasant's Eye **11**
  Summer **11**
Piagle **107**
Pilewort **111**
Pimpernel, Scarlet **11**
  Yellow **103**
Pineapple Weed 75
Pink, Cheddar **16**
  Clove 16
  Deptford **16**
Piss-a-bed **113**
Plantain, Floating Water **58**
  Greater **94**
  Hoary **93**
Policeman's Helmet **31**
Pondweed, Broad-leaved **89**
Poor Man's Weatherglass **11**
Poppy, Common **9**
  Corn **9**
  Field **9**
  Long-headed **9**
  Opium **35**
  Yellow Horned **97**
Poppy Dock **30**
Primrose **107**
  Large-flowered Evening **97**

Rabbit's Meat **80, 81**

Raddish, Wild **99**
Ragged Robin **18**
Ragwort, Common **115**
Ramps **73**
Ramsons **73**
Rape **100**
Ratstail **94**
Reedmace, Great **123**
  Lesser 123
Rest-harrow, Common 34
  Spiny **34**
Ribgrass **93**
Rockrose, Common **108**
Rose, Burnet **66**
  Dog **65**
Rosin **105**
Runch **99**
Rush, Flowering **13**
  Soft **122**

Sage, Meadow **53**
  Wild **94**
  Wood **94**
Sainfoin **33**
St. John's Wort, Common **105**
  Perforate **105**
Satin Flower **63**
Saw-wort 39
Saxifrage, Alternate-leaved Golden **98**
  Meadow 69
  Opposite-leaved Golden 98
  Purple **19**
  Rue-leaved **69**
  Starry **69**
Scabious, Devil's Bit **49**
  Field **49**
Scorpion Grass **46**
Sea Holly **49**
Self Heal **52**
  Cut-leaved 52
  Large-flowered 52
Setter-grass **91**
Setterwort **91**
Shepherd's Purse **61**
Shepherd's Weatherglass **11**
Shirt Buttons **63**
Silverweed **102**
Skullcap, Common **51, 52**
  Lesser 51
Snake Root **22**
Snake's Head **37**
Snake Weed **22**
Snow Bell **73**
Snowdrop **72**
Snow-in-Summer 63
Soapwort 17, **21**

Soldiers **93**
Solomon's Seal, Angular 77
  Common **77**
  Whorled 77
Sorrel **8**
  Mountain **88**
  Sheep's **8**
  Wood **67**, 72
Sour Sauce **8**
Sowthistle, Common **115**
  Prickly 115
Spearworts 104
Speedwell, Common **43**
  Heath **43**
  Rock **44**
  Shrubby **44**
  Water 43
Spinach, Wild **86**
Spurge, Caper **83**
  Cypress **83**
  Wood **84**
Spurrey, Corn **64**
  Sand **23**

Sea **23**
Stinking Roger **40**
Stitchwort, Greater **63**
  Lesser 63
Stonecrop, Biting **108**
  Yellow **108**
Strawberry, Barren **67**
  Wild **67**
  Yellow **105**
Succory, Wild **50**
Sundew, Common **71**
Swede **100**

Tare, Hairy 33, **57**
  Smooth 57
Teasel **38**
Thistle, Carline **112**
  Creeping **38**
  Field **38**
Throatwort **55**
Thyme **28**
  Larger Wild 28
Toadflax, Common **119**
  Ivy-leaved **41**

Purple **41**
Tom Thumb **120**
Tormentil **101**
Tulip, Wild **37**
Twayblade, Common **95**

Valerian, Red **31**
Vetch, Kidney **120**
  Tufted 33, **42**
Vine, Wild **68**
Violet, Common Dog **57**
  Sweet 57
  Wood Dog 57

Wallflower **98**
Wall Pepper **108**
Waterblobs **112**
Water-lily, White **112**
  Yellow **112**
Water Soldier **58**
Way-bread **94**
Weasel's Snout **118**
Weeping Widow **37**
Whin **121**

White Goosefoot **85**
Whortleberry **12**
Wild White **79**
Willowherb, Great **14**
  Great Hairy **14**
  Hairy **14**
  Rosebay **14**
Wind Flower **72**
Wintergreen, Common **70**
  Intermediate 70
  Larger 70
Woad **100**
Wolfsbane **47**
Woodbind **117**
Woodbine **117**
Wood Germander **94**
Woundwort, Hedge 27, **39**
  Marsh **27**, 39
  Wood 27, **39**

Yarrow **76**
Yellow Archangel **118**
Yellow Flag **96**
Yellow Rattle **118**

Index of Scientific Names

Page numbers referring to illustrations appear in **bold type**

Achillea millefolium **76**
Aconitum napellus **47**
Adonis aestevalis **11**
  annua **11**
Aegopodium podagraria **81**
Agrostemma githago **17**
Ajuga reptans **51,** 52
Alliaria petiolata **60**
Allium triquetrum **73**
  ursinum **73**
  vineale **29**
Althaea officinalis 21
Anacamptis pyramidalis **32**
Anagallis arvensis **11**
Anemone nemorosa **72**
  ranunculoides 72
Anthriscus sylvestris **80**
Anthyllis vulneraria **120**
Aquilegia vulgaris **56**
Arabis alpina **61**
  caucasica 61
Arum maculatum **88**
Aster novi-belgii **48**
Astrantia major **79**
Atriplex patula **86**
Atropa belladonna **123**

Bellis perennis **74**
Berberis vulgaris **110**
Bilderdykia convolvulus **92**
Borago officinalis **47**
Brassica napus **100**
  nigra 99
Bryonia dioica **68**
Buglossoides purpurocaerulea **46**
Butomus umbellatus **13**

Caltha palustris **110**
Calluna vulgaris **15,** 29
Calystegia sepium **78**
Campanula spp. 55
  rotundifolia **55**
  trachelium **55**
Capsella bursa-pastoris **61**
Cardamine pratensis **15**
Carlina vulgaris **112**
Centaurea cyanus **50**
  nigra **39**
  scabiosa 12
Centaurium erythraea **18**
  tenuiflorum 18
Centranthus ruber **31**
Cephalanthera rubra **24**

Cerastium arvense **63**
  tomentosum 63
Cheiranthus cheiri **98**
Chelidonium majus **101**
Chenopodium album **85**
  bonus-henricus **86**
Chrysanthemum leucanthemum **74**
  segetum **114**
Chrysosplenium alternifolium **98**
  oppositifolium 98
Cichorium intybus **50**
Cirsium arvense **38**
Consolida ambigua **56**
  orientalis 56
  regalis 56
Convallaria majalis **78**
Cornus suecica **35**
Cymbalaria muralis **41**
Cynoglossum germanicum 10
  officinale **10**
Cytisus scoparius **121**

Dactylorhiza fuchsii 32
Daucus carota **82**
Dianthus armeria **16**

  caryophyllus 16
  gratianopolitanus **16**
Digitalis purpurea **30**
Dipsacus fullonum **38**
Drosera spp. 71
  rotundifolia **71**

Echium vulgare **54**
Epilobium angustifolium **14**
  hirsutum **14**
Epipactis atrorubens 24
Erica cinerea **29**
  tetralix 29
Eryngium maritimum **49**
Eupatorium cannabinum **25**
Euphorbia amygdaloides **84**
  cyparissias **83**
  lathyrus **83**
Euphrasia officinalis **77**

Filipendula ulmaria **71**
  vulgaris 71
Fragaria vesca **67**
Fritillaria meleagris **37**
Fumaria capreolata 30
  muralis 30
  officinalis **30**

parviflora 30

Galanthus nivalis **72**
Galega officinalis **33**
Galium aparine **59**
  spurium 59
Gentiana verna **45**
  nivalis 45
Geranium pratense **45**
  purpureum 20
  pyrenaicum 20
  robertianum 20
  sanguineum **10**
  sylvaticum 45
Geum rivale **20**
  urbanum **105**
Glaucium flavium **97**
Glechoma hederacea 51, **52**
Gymnadenia conopsea 32

Helianthemum nummularium **108**
Helleborus foetidus **91**
  viridis **91**
Hepatica nobilis **48**
Heracleum mantegazzianum 81
  sphondylium **81**
Hieracium aurantiacum **12**
Himantoglossum hircinum **95**
Humulus lupulus **92**
Hyacinthoides non-scripta **54**
Hydrocharis morsus-ranae **59**
Hypericum perforatum **105**

Iberis amara **60**
Impatiens capensis 31
  glandulifera **31**
  noli-tangere 31
Iris pseudacorus **96**
Isatis tinctoria **100**

Juncus effusus **122**

Knautia arvensis **49**

Lamiastrum galeobdolon **118**
Lamium album **76**
  maculatum 76
Lathyrus latifolius 34
  sylvestris **34**
Leucanthemum vulgare 74
Limonium humile 36
  vulgare **36**
Linaria purpurea **41**
  vulgaris **119**

Listera ovata **95**
Lonicera periclymenum **117**
Lotus corniculatus **120**
Luronium natans **58**
Lychnis flos-cuculi **18**
Lysimachia nemorum **103**
  nummularia **103**
  vulgaris **106**
Lythrum salicaria **24**

Malva moschata 21
  sylvestris **21**
Matricaria matricarioides 75
  recutita **75**
Medicago sativa 33, **42**
Melampyrum pratense **117**
Mentha spp. 28
Mercurialis annua 84
  perennis **84**
Myosotis arvensis **46**

Narcissus pseudonarcissus **109**
Narthecium ossifragum **109**
Nuphar lutea **112**
Nymphaea alba **112**

Odontites verna **26**
Oenanthe pimpinelloides **82**
Oenothera erythrosepala **97**
Onobrychis viciifolia **33**
Ononis repens 34
  spinosa **34**
Ophrys apifera **26**
  fuciflora 26
  insectifera 26
Orchis mascula **32**
Origanum vulgare **28**
Oxalis acetosella **67,** 72
Oxyria digyna **88**

Papaver dubium **9**
  rhoeas **9**
  somniferum **35**
Parietaria diffusa **87**
Paris quadrifolia **90**
Pastinaca sativa **122**
Pentaglottis sempervirens 43
Petasites fragrans 25
  hybridus **25**
Pinguicula lusitanica 103
  vulgaris **40**
Plantago lanceolata **93**
  major **94**
  media **93**
Polygonatum multiflorum 77

odoratum 77
  verticillatum 77
Polygonum aviculare **23**
  bistorta **22**
  viviparum **70**
Potamogeton natans **89**
Potentilla anserina **102**
  erecta **101**
  reptans **102**
  sterilis **67**
Primula veris **107**
  vulgaris **107**
Prunella grandiflora 52
  laciniata 52
  vulgaris **52**
Pulicaria dysenterica **116**
Pulsatilla vulgaris **36**
Pyrola media 70
  minor **70**
  rotundifolia 70

Ranunculus acris **104**
  aquatilis **65**
  bulbosus 104
  ficaria **111**
  flammula 104
  repens **104**
Raphanus raphanistrum **99**
Rhinanthus minor **118**
Rosa canina **65**
  pimpinellifolia **66**
Rubus fruticosus **66**
Rumex acetosa **8**
  acetosella **8**
  obtusifolius **89**

Salvia horminoides 53
  pratensis **53**
Sanguisorba officinalis **37**
Saponaria officinalis 17, **21**
Saxifraga granulata 69
  oppositifolia **19**
  stellaris **69**
  tridactylites **69**
Scrophularia aquatica 40
  nodosa **40**
Scutellaria galericulata **51,** 52
  minor 51
Sedum acre **108**
  telephium **22**
Senecio jacobaea **115**
  sylvaticus **113**
  viscosus 113
  vulgaris 113
Serratula tinctoria 39
Silene acaulis **19**
  alba **62**
  dioica **17,** 21

vulgaris **62**
Sisymbrium officinale **99**
Solanum dulcamara **123**
  nigrum **68**
  sarrachoides 68
Solidago virgaurea **116**
Sonchus asper 115
  oleraceus **115**
Spartium junceum 121
Spergula arvensis **64**
Spergularia marina 23
  rubra **23**
Stachys officinalis **27**
  palustris **27,** 39
  sylvatica 27, **39**
Stellaria graminea 63
  holostea **63**
  media **64**
Stratiotes aloides **58**
Succisa pratensis **49**
Symphytum officinale **53**

Tamus communis **90**
Tanacetum parthenium **75**
Taraxacum vulgare **113**
Teucrium scorodonia **94**
Thalictrum flavum **96**
Thymus pulegioides 28
  serpyllum **28**
Torilis japonica **80**
Trifolium incarnatum **13**
  pratense **13**
  repens **79**
Trollius europaeus **111**
Tulicaria vulgaris 116
Tussilago farfara **114**
Typha angustifolia 123
  latifolia **123**

Ulex europaeus **121**
Urtica dioica **85**

Vaccinium myrtillus **12**
Verbascum thapsus **106**
Veronica anagallis-aquatica 43
  beccabunga **43**
  fruticans **44**
  officinalis **43**
Vicia cracca 33, **42**
  hirsuta 33, **57**
  tetrasperma 57
Vinca major 44
  minor **44**
Viola arvensis 119
  odorata 57
  reichenbachiana 57
  riviniana **57**
  tricolor **119**
Viscum album **87**

128